T0193695

OUTRIGHT CHANGES
IN AN OUTRAGEOUS WORLD

6 STEPS TO ACTIVATING LASTING
CHANGE DURING YOUR DARKEST DAYS

CASSANDRA BURKART

BALBOA.PRESS

A DIVISION OF HAY HOUSE

This book is a work of non-fiction. Unless otherwise noted, the author and the publisher make no explicit guarantees as to the accuracy of the information contained in this book and in some cases, names of people and places have been altered to protect their privacy.

Balboa Press books may be ordered through booksellers or by contacting:

Balboa Press
A Division of Hay House
1663 Liberty Drive
Bloomington, IN 47403
www.balboapress.com
844-682-1282

Because of the dynamic nature of the Internet, any web addresses or links contained in this book may have changed since publication and may no longer be valid. The views expressed in this work are solely those of the author and do not necessarily reflect the views of the publisher, and the publisher hereby disclaims any responsibility for them.

The author of this book does not dispense medical advice or prescribe the use of any technique as a form of treatment for physical, emotional, or medical problems without the advice of a physician, either directly or indirectly. The intent of the author is only to offer information of a general nature to help you in your quest for emotional and spiritual well-being. In the event you use any of the information in this book for yourself, which is your constitutional right, the author and the publisher assume no responsibility for your actions.

Print information available on the last page.

ISBN: 979-8-7652-2547-9 (sc)
ISBN: 979-8-7652-2549-3 (hc)
ISBN: 979-8-7652-2548-6 (e)

Library of Congress Control Number: 2022911507

Balboa Press rev. date: 08/01/2022

CONTENTS

ACKNOWLEDGMENTS

I cannot express enough gratitude and appreciation for my friends, family, coaches, and mentors in my life that have supported and encouraged me along my journey.

I want to thank the incredible parents who raised me to be a woman of strength and independence. Your example of perseverance showed me what it looks like to achieve greatness through unwavering commitments.

Next, I want to thank my sisters for their continued support, compassion, and love. I will always treasure my relationship with you girls, as you are the connecting link to my youth and childhood memories.

Lastly, but most importantly, I want to express the utmost gratitude to my loving and supportive husband, Kelsey. You have been my most tremendous encouragement throughout my journey, giving me the strength and courage to reach for self-fulfillment each and every day.

INTRODUCTION

On January 9th, 2020, panic and fear spread across the globe. The announcement came from the World Health Organization (WHO) that a mysterious Coronavirus was identified in Wuhan, China. This flu-like virus spread rapidly, and by January 21st, 2020, it made its way to North America. The rapid transmission and, at the time, what appeared to be a high-rate infectious disease, placed the entire world, including our family, into a state of ultimate chaos, full of fear. By March 11th, the WHO declared COVID-19 to be a pandemic, as it met these three requirements: sustained person-to-person transmission, a disease resulting in death, and lastly, worldwide infection. Shortly after declaring a pandemic status, the world began to shut down. On March 12th, Canada announced the closure of schools, sports leagues, non-essential services, and the government. Closure of the Canadian border followed this; only Canadian residents were permitted into the country. Businesses closed their doors, people lost their jobs, and ultimately, families were torn apart. The globe experienced this tragic outcome, not just here in North America. The chain of events happened so fast that no one knew what to expect next. There was limited data available as to what COVID-19 was capable of, leading to the worst possible outcomes embedded into the minds of all.

Fear took over our communities, leaving people feeling lost, afraid, and alone. Anxiety, stress, and depression spiked to all-time highs, leaving most of us feeling like we were losing control of our lives. We lost loved ones to mental health issues, and thousands died from the Coronavirus. Division and separation began to creep into our society as individuals had unique values and made different choices. Numerous people feared the COVID-19 virus and chose to take the experimental vaccines, while some feared the vaccines and chose not to get vaccinated. Others developed fears of losing the ability to make decisions for themselves as the mandates and restrictions intensified. What was the outcome of all of this? Our basic, psychological and self-fulfilling needs became threatened, leaving our globe in a state of judgment, hate, criticism, blame, and all of this ego-driven environment's hostile actions and attitudes. Individuals slipped from their thriving and prosperous states into survival and scarcity mode.

Observing the pain and suffering many individuals endured throughout the Coronavirus pandemic, it is important to recognize moments of anguish have always existed, even before the shutdown of our world. We can view the COVID-19 experience as a magnifier to the darkness that already existed; now, many more individuals have been impacted, resulting in a collective state of distress. This broad impact and shared experience can bring a deeper understanding of the anguish that has always penetrated society. This extensive impact is why I have chosen the Coronavirus pandemic as the case study throughout this book. As we consider the questions many individuals ask because of their hurt during COVID-19, we can recognize the validity of these inquiries at any moment. These thoughts and queries include: is it possible to continue to advance towards abundance as the chains of fear take over? Is there a way to rebuild ourselves to inspire boldness, courage, and peace within? Can we get to a place where we can accept the outcomes that have transpired and begin to move forward?

I wholeheartedly believe we can. My belief is strong because my family experienced painful infringements on our needs throughout COVID-19, leading to anxiety, depression, fears, and judgments. We came out on the other end more enlightened and unified than ever before, making significant strides towards our greatest hopes and desires. Did we all share the same journey and fears? No! Some individuals developed substantial concerns about the COVID-19 virus, others developed fears of the vaccines, and some of us feared losing our freedom of choice. We all experienced different fears, preferences, and outcomes. This personalized approach to the hardships experienced shaped the unique paths we each walked upon. Individuality within my family has always existed, even before the pandemic outbreak. The same can be said about the uniqueness embedded within society. Whether someone's darkest days are during the COVID-19 pandemic or occur outside of this time, individuals will always make different choices supported by unique values. These differences will always exist, leading to the question of how do we get through the judgments, criticisms, and anger with one another? How do we become unified while being rooted in our differences?

The rest of this book will share six fundamental principles that anyone can apply to elevate and grow towards their highest potential, including during chaotic times like the Coronavirus pandemic. You will learn about the importance of establishing your purpose, fueled by a burning desire to transform your life. A part of this transformation journey will require you to take an inventory of your past to gain clarity of your present. While you build this transparency and understanding of your current moments in time, you will acquire the courage to take complete ownership of your life. Through this crucial step of accepting accountability, your courage will propel you to take action, moving towards your goals and ultimate self-fulfillment. As you begin to take these steps forward, you will face obstacles and roadblocks, potentially hindering your progression. You will learn about some of the common hindrances individuals experience and how to overcome those present in your life. To ensure you are advancing in the direction of your aspirations, you will discover the value of completing regular assessments of your life and your actions.

Through this journey, your personal growth will eradicate the negative thoughts, emotions, fears, actions, and ultimately adverse outcomes you are experiencing. You will unlock the hidden potential that already exists within you while creating lasting and positive changes in your life. As each individual chooses to live at their best, elevating to their higher selves, they will positively impact their surroundings and people within these environments. You will become a profound influencer as your transformations will also elevate your family, friends, acquaintances, communities, and nations. As you lead your growth journey in life, you too can influence others to lead their own. Your commitment to choosing unity over ego will contribute to the unification our world desperately needs. Only then can you begin to live a life of ultimate and holistic fulfillment.

CHAPTER 1

Purpose Fueled by a Burning Desire

Your Inspiration

Before we understand how one grows and develops during turbulent times, such as during the Coronavirus pandemic, I think it is essential to reflect on why you are reading this book. Is it because you desire to make changes in your own life? Are you experiencing challenges, leading to a blurred vision and lost purpose? Or perhaps you are looking for guidance as a traumatic event has forever altered the trajectory of your life. Whichever your reasons for picking up this book, I hope you experience the enlightenment you are searching for as you continue towards your self-fulfillment. The tools presented here will be transformational for any turbulence; identifying your personal "why" will only make the methods more effective in your life.

Personal Inspiration

My inspiration for writing this book came when I experienced an awareness of the toxic state our world has fallen into. Our nations were in a state of scarcity, fear, and separation before the pandemic. My understanding of this condition did not occur until things became magnified by the darkness that ensued during COVID-19. Many individuals were ignorant and unaware of the toxicity that seeped within our homes, myself included. For many, COVID-19 was the magnifying glass held over existing problems. For example, individuals struggled with their faith, mental and physical health, financial management, and healthy relationships before the pandemic. The devastation from COVID led to some questioning their faith, and isolation and stress from the unknowns exasperated mental and physical health concerns. Those with underlying health conditions experienced a more significant threat from the virus. Those who were already struggling with finances endured enhanced financial pressures. Before the pandemic, those experiencing relationship issues had these concerns exasperated with additional stresses and isolation. Through my realization, I knew in my heart that things needed to desperately change to have the peace, freedom, and unification we all desire. Leading up to writing this book, I passionately pursued numerous years of personal growth and development combined with being a coach and mentor to others. As a coach over the last five years, my passion resides in helping others grow in every area of their life, elevating their faith, calling or career, finances, health, and relationships. Through my guidance, I have helped numerous individuals elevate in all of these critical areas leading to the ultimate fulfillment of one's life. The methods I use as a coach has proven successful in my life and the lives of others. I will expand on these methods throughout this book, detailing the six steps to activating lasting change. My intention in sharing my philosophy is pure, with the desire to profoundly impact the state of our world. In our journey together, I will pull apart the curtains, displaying the truths of how one individual's commitment towards elevation can impact the condition of our entire globe. That positive, influential person can be you!

A Transformed Life

To positively impact others' lives, I will share my personal story tangled between principles and knowledge I have gained throughout the many years of pursuing coaching and mentoring. I hope that sharing my narrative alongside the concrete methods you can use will humanize our time together. You are just as capable of this transformation as I am. I'll start by taking you back to the day that transformed my life. I met my husband Kelsey, in the fall of 2014, at a fitness and bodybuilding competition. Our meeting was a divinely organized happening that required the elimination of many obstacles for us to meet by chance. Last-minute, Kelsey received approval from his boss to take some vacation time, in which he chose to come to Edmonton to watch a friend of his competing in the fitness competition. On my end, after stepping on stage, my goal was to grab a quick bite to eat and head home after a long day full of exhaustion. My plans changed at the very last minute as a friend invited me out to dinner with a group of her friends. Once arriving at the restaurant, our table contained both competitors and audience members watching the show. It was at that table that I met my future husband, Kelsey. We connected right away, as our values aligned with one another.

Our passionate honeymoon phase transitioned into a very toxic relationship as we began dating. We cared deeply about each other; however, demons from our past hindered the progression of the intimate connection we both desired. I brought a controlling, insensitive, numbing, and insecure nature to the table while he added distrust, anxiety, depression, and self-esteem issues. We were both a hot mess, trying to fill in each other's weaknesses, not recognizing we were only pouring gasoline on the embers that were scorching to touch. It felt as though the roof of our home had collapsed inward, trapping us in these hostile environments that we had created for ourselves.

Fortunately, we both have a stubborn streak; we were not willing to give up on our love for one another. The desire for change and growth burned so intensely that we were ready to do whatever it took to become a unified couple. We both understood that our brains got us into this mess, and it certainly wasn't going to be our brains that would get us out of it. Since we desired holistic growth, we knew that the only way to navigate down this road, one we had never traveled before, was to pursue associations with individuals who have ventured down the paths before us. We searched for leaders within our communities that had a life we desired and shared similar values to ourselves. As we surrounded ourselves more and more with individuals living a value-based life, we quickly learned that we had to eradicate the unhealthy ego in our minds to promote growth and healing. This form of ego wants us to remain in a state of turmoil, making us believe that we know the answers to all of our problems. The reality is that our inner being yearns for deep connections, where we learn and grow from those around us. Over time, my husband and I let down our walls and, with vulnerability, selected a few key individuals who agreed to coach and mentor us in various areas of our life.

The question then became, what made up the non-negotiable values in our life? To grow, we needed to identify the areas of our lives requiring nourishment. Through numerous intimate conversations with one another, we created and solidified our value system, determining the direction we wanted to go. This structure included our faith, relationships, finances, health, and calling. These fundamental values formed the pillars of our home. Each pillar played a significant role and was equally important in ensuring the strength and stability of our home.

As you can see clearly, one cracked or broken pillar can cause strain on the other key pillars of your life. Suppose an individual does nothing to fill in the cracks or rebuild the shattered pillars. In that case, eventually, you will experience a collapse of the entire structure that makes up your purposeful life.

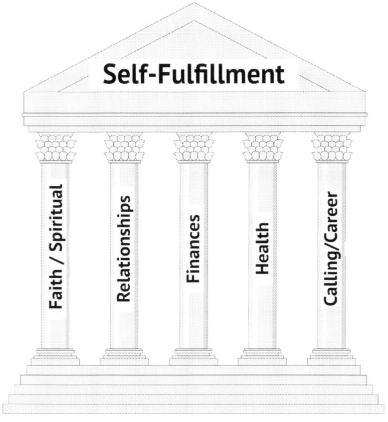

Figure 1: Pillars of Values Leading to a Life Fulfilled

Purpose Fueled by a Burning Desire

With a compass in mind, and navigators to follow, Kelsey and I embarked on one of the most challenging and rewarding journeys we would face. To personalize this journey towards growth, I created my mission statement fueled by my internal burning desires. This proclamation is my ultimate purpose in my life; I knew, even then, that if I were able to live my life in complete alignment with that purpose, I would attain the peace that is available for all if we reach for it. I will share these intimate words below in the hopes that they can inspire you to either reflect upon or identify your values and purpose in this life along with your burning desires. I encourage you to write them down and read them every day to keep you on your path toward fulfillment.

> My ultimate *purpose* is to live a life full of growth and abundance in my faith, relationships, finances, mental & physical health, and calling. My vision is to create a positive impact everywhere I go, leaving a shining light in one soul to the next. My *burning desire* is to grow through the toxicity and fears that take over my life at any given point in time, always realigning to my values, and bringing peace into our home. I desire unity within my family and community and realignment with my higher self, God.

Now, take a moment to think through and write down your own personal mission statement. It's OK if you're not 100% sure yet; you can continue to refine it as we go on this journey together. This personal mission statement is more than just the individual words that make up the paragraph. It is the fuel I need to activate change in my life, using it as a daily affirmation to rewire my thinking processes. As Kelsey and I made up our unique mission statements, speaking to our individual hearts, they contained an identical overarching vision and value system. To be genuinely unified, working towards a shared vision, we needed to feel safe to bring our distinctive characteristics and individuality to the table.

As we started the process of elevating our lives, it became critical to filter our daily decisions through our values system. This conscious decision created an aligned, peaceful, and purposeful life for both my husband and I. Strengthening these pillars revealed the blind spots and areas that required growth. This transformational journey began by eliminating negative habits that were holding us back and replacing them with new habits placing a priority on change. The negative and lower energy inputs we chose to stop include social media, news, ads, movies, and TV. Additionally, we learned the value of being selective with our associations in our life, realizing the collection of our connections makes up who we are as individuals. We lovingly chose to set boundaries and limit our time with those individuals who did not support our goals and values through this realization. Relationships are a vital pillar in our lives, so it was essential for us to communicate with love and affection as we put these new boundaries in place. A crucial component to ensure lasting change in eliminating a bad habit is replacing these old ways with new positive behaviors. For Kelsey and I, this included reaching out to the coaches and mentors in our life regularly for guidance, reading personal growth books for fifteen to thirty minutes a day, listening to an educational podcast or audiobook each day, eating healthy and exercising regularly, and budgeting and living below our means. We recognized that if one of our key pillars became weak or broken, this hindrance put more pressure on all other areas of our lives. As you continue to read below, I will share more intimately with you the changes that I needed to walk through to become the best version of myself. Only then could I be a contributor to the unified vision I shared with my husband. I will offer these using the structure of my personal "pillars" in the hopes that it helps you identify the pillars that are important in your self-growth journey.

Faith

I always knew a higher power existed throughout my younger years, but I did not look at God or Source as a part of all things. Being raised Catholic, the religious indoctrinations led me to believe that God was a figurehead sitting up in heaven. Religious leaders expressed that I needed to act according to God's laws to go to heaven. This belief never sat right with me because I knew that God does not partake in favoritism, bribe, or manipulate you to behave in a certain way. Because of the religious exposures I experienced, I leaned away from my faith. I soon felt incredibly lost in the regular cycle of getting up, going to work, coming home, and repeating the process the next day. I wasn't sure what was missing in my life, but I knew that something was not right. I became consumed with finding the next goal to fill the void I was sensing. I eventually felt my thoughts sinking into self-judgment, criticism, and comparison. I kept repeating, "there has to be something more than this. What is wrong with me? What am I missing?"

After getting married, these feelings of living a life absent of meaning escalated. How could I be the best version of myself for my husband if I didn't even know where I stood with my faith? Eventually, feeling so absent, I realized the need for change. On the journey to self-fulfillment, my personal growth sparked my curiosity, and my desire to understand what I truly believed inspired my spiritual quest. Using the newfound leaders in my life to guide me, I turned to podcasts and books from various spiritual individuals with a Christian background. I hoped that by learning from others and hearing their personal experiences, I would find something that would resonate. I truly desired to experience this "knowing of God" however, I can honestly say that the more I surrounded myself with faithful individuals, the more I became increasingly confused about what I truly believed. The path to strengthening my faith pillar was in its infancy before the pandemic outbreak. I did not know then that there were cracks within the walls of my faith pillar and that those cracks would contribute to the unfortunate events that unfolded during COVID-19.

Relationships

Within my relationship values, Kelsey and I prioritized four levels of relationships in our lives. In order of importance, these levels include marriage, children, extended family, and other meaningful relationships. There is a sequential order to prioritize growth within these relationships to flourish.

Marriage

The most important relationship outside of the one with God is the one between partners. Our marriage is the first level within our relationship pillar that requires our utmost attention and priority. For a solid marriage to develop, we learned that we needed to take care of our personal needs while elevating towards our higher selves. Only then can we add value to the entirety of our relationship. We needed to advance towards being the best version of ourselves before we could be the best version for each other. An important component to recognize is that you cannot expect both individuals in a relationship to be in the same book, let alone on the same page. We are all uniquely designed and have our own stories that makeup who we are. It is imperative, though, to have commonality within a partnership. Recognizing this, Kelsey and I placed a high value on developing a shared vision to establish.

This revolutionary way of thinking was not how we lived our lives. Society tells us that for a relationship to work, you need to be on the same page; you need to be very similar in every aspect.

It is no wonder marriages are set up for failure, as we expect others to be just like us. These expectations go against the design of humanity as no two humans are exactly alike, not even identical twins. Although identical twins share the same genetic code, they embody uniqueness within their environmental exposures, influencing the mind and body differently. This desire that many individuals hold, expecting their partners to be their duplicates, leads to actions of control, desires to change one another, and can even lead to manipulation. These actions create the toxic environment many couples find themselves in, including my husband and me. We entered our relationship with the desire to mold one another, as we thought a healthy marriage meant we needed to have the same goals, values, and personalities.

Once Kelsey and I understood the need for our individuality, we went to work on transforming ourselves. We read personal growth and marriage books, listened to audiobooks and podcasts, and prioritized learning from individuals who created successful marriages. As simple as this sounds, our relationship required immense work. I learned to let down my rigid exterior walls to become open to change and growth with my husband. The by-product of this created a safe space for me to show emotion and sensitivity, further contributing to a growing relationship. I also had to learn to let others lead, in this case, my husband. This willingness to accept his leadership does not mean I gave up making decisions; instead, I learned to trust and respect Kelsey's thoughts and choices. This process of embracing his guidance created a space where Kelsey learned to respect and trust my thoughts and intentions in return. It was also crucial to the health of our relationship that I learned to prioritize my time towards my values and eliminate pursuing numbing activities. Before deciding to change and work on me, I was addicted to the busyness of life and never let myself slow down. At the time, I prioritized activities and accomplishments, even if they did not align with my purpose. I intended to keep my mind busy from the many problems that lay dormant. These actions contributed to the disconnection and lack of empathy towards all relationships, especially with Kelsey. By focusing on my values and removing that busyness, I became more connected and welcomed my desired transformation and growth.

As I was opening myself up in our relationship, Kelsey was walking through different anxieties while working on building trust and self-worth. For Kelsey to trust and love others, including myself, he first had to establish faith and love within himself. As they say, you cannot give what you don't have. Through this growth process, Kelsey learned to have faith in his abilities, creating the confidence he needed to step up and lead himself and our home. Kelsey and I began to live a healthy and prosperous marriage for the first time. Our unification became so intense that we could finally face all obstacles as a team. This unity was the foundation for creating change in all the other pillars within our value system.

Parenting

Looking at the second level of our relationship pillar, this is where our children and future grandchildren reside. In the early stages of our relationship, this level was non-existent; however, we always had conversations about the value of these relationships. By the time Kelsey and I chose to have children, we were about three years into our elevation journey. We had grown through most of the toxicity in our relationship and strengthened the other pillars in our life. We unveiled our most genuine callings by eliminating our lives' egos and false identifications. For me, a true calling that I had been denying was becoming a mom and being able to stay home and raise my kids. Having the courage to say no to a career and the accolades that came with it relieved the immense societal pressure that I felt. It was as if my firm boundaries had lifted an enormous weight off my shoulders. At first, receiving many comments, concerns, and even criticisms, I questioned my decision. However, intuitively I knew Chemical Engineering was not my purpose; my destiny was to be a mom actively raising my kids. By following my values and making the right decisions for my family, I found the peace and joy essential to living an authentic, wholehearted life.

When our first child Benson was born, we had built a solid foundation of healthy habits while maintaining a solid support group. We were well equipped to learn the intricacies of parenthood. Choosing to continue the practices of positive input, including reading parenting books and listening to audiobooks and podcasts, was instrumental in our parenting growth journey. As most parents know, there is no exact method or means for raising children, and, at times, parents can find themselves overwhelmed with the varying stages of child-rearing. With these positive and developmental habits that we implemented while raising our first child, we felt equipped to bring our second child, Brooklyn, into the world. As expected, our journey of raising Brooklyn was very different from that of raising Benson, as no two children are alike. While continuing down this path of parenthood, growth and development must remain a priority, as our children learn a great deal from the examples we set before them.

Extended Family

Our extended family includes our parents, siblings, grandparents, and other relatives apart from our family tree. These important relationships make up the third level within our relationship pillar. Both Kelsey and I were fortunate to have parents who we considered strong role models in our lives during our upbringing. Both of our parents were committed to their marriages, showing us what it looks like to stay committed to one another, no matter what challenges they faced. Their unwavering commitment transcended into the fabric of our beings. By their example, the insistent nature Kelsey and I exhibited within our marriage was the key to unlocking the intimacy and strength that our union needed to thrive. This determination guided us to let down our egos and allow others to speak into our lives.

In addition to my loving parents, I have two siblings that I was close to growing up. I have a twin sister, Kayla, who I was inseparable from, and I have a younger sister, Chantelle, who I was close to during various stages of our upbringing. Throughout our adolescent years, we three girls did everything together. Things began to change as Kayla, and I entered our teenage years. We started a different stage of our life, leaving Chantelle behind. These differences led to a significant amount of turmoil between us three girls. It was understandable that Chantelle began to feel inadequate and excluded, developing resentment and anger toward Kayla and me. During this period of our lives, Chantelle and I formed an unhealthy relationship that endured for many years. Only when I embarked on my transformational journey did the healing process begin. I learned from those around me who had healthy relationships. I obtained clarity on my blind spots, taking ownership of my contribution to the toxicity that entered the sacred relationship between sisters. Chantelle and I finally began to put together our broken relationship.

Growing up with a twin sister also came with its challenges. Kayla and I were essentially living as identical human beings because we did everything together, attended the same classes, participated in the same sports, and had the same friends. We felt incomplete when we were apart, lacking the courage and self-esteem to be our authentic selves. The problem with trying to be the same is that, by nature, we are two very different individuals with unique passions and personalities. We both felt our true and individual natures held caged to conform to the identity of being a twin. As we entered high school, we decided to pursue individuality for the first time in our teenage years. We attended different classes and developed our own circle of friends. This decision to go out on our own brought many painful moments wrapped up in egotism. We experienced frustration, comparison, jealousy, resentment, and anger toward one another as everything did turn into a competition. We both felt as though we were losing ourselves since all we ever knew was who we were as one. We didn't realize that this immense tension resulted from our authentic selves beginning to emerge. This disconnection and disunity our relationship experienced lasted nearly ten years until we decided to seek guidance from outside individuals to help heal our fractured relationship. I needed to take accountability for my contributions to the brokenness we both felt while applying forgiveness for hurtful actions and outcomes that transpired. My twin sister and I have discovered the beauty of becoming our true selves for the first time. We accepted that the abundance we each bring to our relationship is because of our uniqueness. This acceptance was the moment we became uniquely connected.

Other Meaningful Relationships

For Kelsey and I, the fourth level in our relationship pillar includes other meaningful relationships such as friends, acquaintances, and even strangers. We enhanced our understanding of the value of relationships when we let down our walls and let others in, specifically our coaches and mentors. This vulnerability meant being open to receiving and giving within the dynamic relationships between client and coach. The results we experienced from this openness were life-altering. We quickly realized a component of fulfillment in one's life is about who you know rather than what you know. We discovered that everyone who enters our life, whether for a moment, a season, or a lifetime, is there to teach us something.

This appreciation that Kelsey and I have for connections today did not always exist. Before seeking guidance from others, I did not value developing other meaningful relationships. The way I lived my life before I invested myself in growth and development involved building false relationships out of ego instead of love. I saw myself as separate from others and my environment. I looked at everything as a competition, where one person or thing won while others lost. During this time, I thought failure was unspeakable and should be avoided. You were either right or wrong, and being wrong meant you failed. I believed that conquering others was required to achieve my goals. Dichotomies ruled my thinking process. Outcomes of good vs. evil, right vs. wrong, smart vs. dumb, strong vs. weak, beautiful vs. ugly, nice vs. mean, and many more fueled the segregation I felt. Because of these negative thought complexes, the relationships in my life were built upon the eroded surfaces of judgment, criticism, comparison, and selfishness. As we all know, erosion is detrimental to the stability of a structure, just like ego is detrimental to the strength of relationships. It was no wonder I felt alone and isolated; I allowed my ego to put me there.

It was not until Kelsey, and I opened ourselves up to the network of enlightened individuals around us that we experienced the potency of our associations' influence. In this journey of vulnerability, I chose to eradicate my thoughts of self-importance and replace them with those of love. I took hold of the separation in my life and consciously decided to work towards unity. This desire for connectivity required eliminating the dichotomies present within my cognitive processes, realizing that we are all different in our ways, appearances, and choices. This uniqueness is what brings forth the beauty within this world. Developing this knowing removed the need to compare, defeat, and judge those around me.

Finances

Before meeting my husband, I was consumed with pursuing my Chemical Engineering Degree, which led to a career working with Dow Chemical. Shortly after landing my dream job, I decided to buy my own house at the age of twenty-four. Resultantly I received an abundance of accolades from family and friends. This recognition and the feeling of being noticed fueled my spending habits. As I purchased a fancy sports car, a done-up truck, and other non-essential items, the debt piled up. I maxed out my credit cards and started to live a life that looked good on the outside but was gangrene on the inside. I met my husband, Kelsey, shortly after "setting up" my life, and he, too, lived the same empty lifestyle. He worked as a Power Engineer making a sizable income that fueled his spending habits. The result of our union was two debt-ridden individuals with over $100,000 in consumer debt, undoubtedly leading to stress and anxiety around paying the bills. What would happen if we couldn't make our payments? The immense amount of stress we experienced living paycheck to paycheck began to weigh heavily on all the other pillars of our life.

Once we decided to begin the process of learning from other individuals, more specifically the coaches we had pursued, Kelsey and I began to create a list of financial goals we desired to create. These aspirations included: eliminating all consumer debt, owning our house with no mortgage, diversifying our financial portfolio to create passive income, establishing financial independence, and leaving a legacy behind for our children. Significant goals require radical shifts and changes to be made. The first step for us was to become educated about money management. We learned about the difference between wants and needs, realizing that our materialistic wants put us into debt. We developed the mentality that if we have financial obligations, we have not earned the "wants." Being unified with our vision, we got on the same page with our finances by creating and following a strict budget. To activate and maintain consistency with our budget, we decided to eliminate eating out, stop purchasing material items that were not deemed essential, and halt extracurricular activities that required money. We even stopped all subscriptions, including cable TV.

We were very serious about turning our finances around. It's not necessary, of course, to be this extreme, but we did so because we wanted to tackle our debt head-on and quickly. As I said, a significant change requires a big shift.

To be debt-free, we decided to sell all the fancy possessions we had accumulated. We sold Kelsey's new truck and my new sports car, and we purchased cheap vehicles. We were so committed to the mindset, "if you have debt, you have not earned the freedom to buy the fancy materialistic items." We experienced external negativity from individuals who did not understand why we made our decisions. Ultimately, our family and friends viewed us as less because we sold all our fancy possessions; people thought we were going backward in life. Little did they realize that we were working on the unseen foundation of our financial pillar that would later bring the finical abundance we desired. Because we became so deeply rooted in our values and took our growth very seriously, we were able to resist the opinions of others. By being diligent in our budget and spending, we achieved our consumer debt-free goal within six months, and soon after, we had multiple six figures in our savings account. In Wayne Dyer's words, we learned to "die while we were alive" [1], giving up everything we thought defined us to gain life's most extraordinary possession: ultimate peace and freedom. With these few milestones met, we plan to continue growing; we have significant goals that require a lifetime of growth and change.

Health

Looking at my overall health, I discovered that two very different components contributed to my overall well-being, my mental and physical health. These areas are intimately connected; therefore, to experience ultimate health, they both must be grown and developed.

Mental Health

If you recall earlier, I opened up about my childhood and the experiences of growing up with my twin sister, Kayla. I was inauthentically living my life for all my adolescent and teenage years, suppressing my true authentic self. By forming my identity primarily around being a twin, I accepted that who I am is partly my own body and partly someone else's. This misidentification is a complex form of egotism where I have tied my self-worth to the label of being a twin. Breaking free from these egoic thoughts meant that I must give up the idea that my reputation or body defines me. Accepting I am not my physique or a given label, I will achieve the severance from these misidentifications. Only then will I attain the autonomy to embrace my authentic nature, where my body is viewed as the house that holds my true self, my soul. Not understanding this at the time, I allowed the label of being a twin to dictate my thoughts, actions, and, resultantly, my outcomes.

The impact of this ongoing cognitive cycle for both Kayla and I led to a dependency on others, a lack of self-confidence, a poor self-image, and no self-esteem. Because we both experienced these negative thoughts and emotions at such a young age, we became known as shy, removed, or disconnected from others. Our timid behaviors led to one of the most painful experiences as we entered middle school: bullying. I could remember being teased because of our red curly hair, big blue eyes, clothes, and how we walked and talked. I accepted these words as the truth at such a young and impressionable age. I, too, began to judge and criticize my physique and appearance. Words like ugly, disgusting, and nasty became branded into my thoughts. Because my inner world became such a dark and hurtful place, I did whatever I could to avoid being still with my thoughts. I became addicted to numbing my mind through the busyness of achievement and accomplishment, and I could not and would not slow down; it was too painful.

Not until meeting my husband and choosing to elevate my life through mentorship did I realize my addiction to being busy. I became aware that my inability to slow down was, in fact, my way of trying to fill the void of the hurt and pains from my past. Experiencing a hindrance to the need for love and belonging through my adolescent years was a yearning I was trying to fulfill. If it were not for my coach, who held up a mirror to my blind spots, revealing the components holding me back, I genuinely do not know where I would be today. I will reiterate it here; my thinking got me to where I was, living life trapped in a mental cage. Like a captured lion, it takes an outside force to open the door towards freedom, so it also requires an outside influence to unlock the mental cages we all put ourselves in.

One of the first things my mentor guided me towards was identifying the roots of my thinking. I began to walk the painful and emotional path of my past with the intention of discovery. Once I revealed the historical wounds and diagnosed the cause, I could then begin the process of acceptance, taking ownership, and healing. This transformation required me to acknowledge the power of my thoughts, understanding that my internal dialogue leads to my responses, actions, and outcomes in life. If I can control my mental processes, I can control my experiences. Rewiring my thinking habits by replacing the negative thoughts with positive and encouraging ones became my focus. Different ways a person can influence their minds are:

- Writing affirmations.
- Listening to personal growth videos and podcasts.
- Reading developmental and uplifting books.
- Surrounding themselves with positive and encouraging individuals.

I needed to implement these positive influential habits in combination with eradicating the negative inputs every day to create a lasting transition. Over time, I shifted my thoughts of fear, pain, blame, anger, and hate towards those of a positive nature. My beliefs adopted the thoughts of faith, healing, ownership, acceptance, and love.

Physical Health

By the time I entered my first year of university, I was severely uncomfortable and self-conscious about my body. I had hit a low with my self-image, believing I was not good enough. While looking in the mirror, I would only see imperfections, the components my peers teased me about through junior high and high school. I couldn't remember the last time I looked at myself and felt love. This moment was a turning point for me; I was tired of sitting around in my misery, waiting for things to get better. I decided to make some radical changes in my life, pursuing a healthier lifestyle involving dieting and regular exercise regimes. Because I had not personally grown what was inside of me yet, I had approached this newfound goal by applying the numbing tactics I had used up to this point in my life. I was addicted to the accolades and busyness that new endeavors would provide, as you have learned. It wasn't long before I decided to take my fitness to the next level, pursuing competitive bodybuilding competitions for the next two years. I saw the fruit of hard work, and after taking home first place in my division at the entry-level of the sport, I became hooked. I moved on to provincials, which became my sole focus. As you are aware, this was when I met my husband, Kelsey.

My relationships with myself, my family, and most importantly, my husband suffered due to my addiction to success. I had put everything on the back burner as I became consumed with self-importance. Eventually, my self-worth got wrapped up in my physical appearance and my success and failures on stage. I allowed my negative thoughts to create a fertile environment for my ego to take control. I became so focused on comparing my body to others and judging my physique that I forgot to appreciate the physical results I achieved through hard work and dedication. This habitual way of criticizing myself and others seeped into all areas of my life, not just the physical. As hard as it is to admit, I realized that I started to judge individuals based on their possessions, successes, and results in life. I am not proud of this time, and I know that I am 100% responsible for these thoughts that I entertained.

Eventually, the success and accolades were not enough to numb my mind and the negative feelings. I turned to another source, food. There is this stigma in the fitness world that you should look lean and muscular 100% of the time, and if you don't, you have let yourself go. After one of my competitions, I could remember that a family friend commented, "I thought you were a fitness competitor; what happened to your abs?" This comment was a stab at my self-image. You are expected to look and behave a certain way. The message pumped into every competitor's brain is "diet diet diet ." Eventually, these external expectations took a toll on my mental processes, leading to my unhealthy relationship with food. I became so ashamed of consuming foods outside of my diet that I would feel uncomfortable eating in front of my friends, family, and husband. This shame led to my secretive behavior of hiding chocolate bars, cookies, and chips throughout the house, consuming them when I was alone. After gaining about thirty pounds, I realized the severity of my eating habits; I could not continue down this path I was on. Neither the extreme of bodybuilding and its associated diets and training regimens nor the extreme of hiding nutrient-poor foods around the house and eating a ton was healthy.

With the support of my husband and the newfound influences in my life, I began the most private and intimate part of my journey, developing self-love for who I am and not for my appearance. The first action I needed to take was to dispel the physical egotism that took hold, which required eliminating the competitive bodybuilding lifestyle from my path. I also had to put up a shield between myself and the connections and friendships I had built while a part of this lifestyle. They were a constant feed into my ego-filled thoughts of self-importance. Once I elevated my environment and made changes to my associations, I embarked on my journey of developing self-love, independent of my physique. I leaned heavily on my coaches and mentors, positive affirmations, developmental audios, and personal growth books every day. Here, the process of altering my cognitive processes was critical in rewriting the narrative I had ingrained in my subconscious mind. I continuously affirmed, "I am beautiful as I was created. We are all unique in our expressions, appearance, and personalities." In unison with eliminating the negative inputs, I continued with a regular exercise regime, but I set boundaries with myself this time. I limited my weightlifting while mixing in more running, yoga, and stretching to ensure physical and mental health. As the years passed, while diligently working on my thought processes combined with healthy exercising, my physical body began to heal, and my internal dialogue shifted from shame to love. I overcame my food addictions, and I am incredibly grateful to share that I can now enjoy a piece of chocolate in the presence of loved ones without feeling guilty. I can confidently say, I now feel an abundance of love for myself.

Career and Calling

As you have learned, I passionately pursued a Chemical Engineering degree because, at the time, my dream job was to become an engineer. My internal motivation for this was inspired by the desire to live a financially abundant life. Later, I recognized that my heart wanted to move in a different direction; I wanted to be a stay-at-home mom. As Kelsey and I built an abundant lifestyle while strengthening our key pillars, I was afforded the option to step away from my career and pursue being home with my kids. While living through this desire of mine, I began to feel the emotions of peace, harmony, and true alignment to my calling. It was this absolute knowing that I had achieved a state of true fulfillment that allowed me to recognize that many individuals are living an unfulfilled life in disharmony. This realization spurred the beginnings of my next burning desire; I wanted to help others achieve their ultimate calling and self-fulfillment as I have. Passionately, I pursued coaching and mentoring, assisting individuals in elevating all the key pillars of their life. As I continue down the path of being a guiding light for others, five years after the inception of this burning desire, this book is written to continue fulfilling my heart's motivation: to make a profound impact in the lives of others.

Summary

The day that transformed my life was the day that Kelsey walked into it. Our meeting, by chance, opened my eyes and heart to the false life I had been living. This divine intervention was the component my life needed to break the chains of addiction and ego that held me captive. As Kelsey and I chose to cultivate and develop ourselves in alignment with our values, our key pillars making up the foundation of our home grew in strength. This stability we strived for only came with time and patience over the six years of being coached and mentored. Enduring and walking through the hardships we had experienced inspired the need to help others; I was destined to be a coach and mentor.

The purpose of sharing my transformation journey is to show you that regardless of your past or where you come from, what pains or hurts you have endured, you too can radically transform your life. As you establish your key pillars, you will find direction and purpose. I encourage you to take a moment to solidify your values and write out your personal mission statement that encompasses these pillars that you hold dear. Use this declaration as your affirmation to maintain alignment with who you desire to be. You may be surprised by the light that this affirmation can bring into your life during moments of darkness. I know I sure was surprised at the impact of my affirmation when COVID 19 occurred.

With all these years of experience being coached in combination with coaching others, I thought Kelsey and I would be able to withstand any strong wind that blew our way until COVID 19 wreaked havoc on our lives. This event strained the pillars we had built, cracked the foundation, and led to an ultimate collapse in our life. These fractures revealed the pillars of our life that needed to be fortified even more. It was my mission statement that illuminated the darkness our home fell into. As you keep reading the coming chapters, you will see the value in establishing your personal declaration. You will also learn the importance of taking an inventory of where you are at so you can begin to identify the steps necessary to move towards your mission. By accepting your current realities, you may notice the adversities present. You will learn the value of these hardships and begin to see them as the answer to your prayers. The ONLY way to elevate towards your highest self is by going through the valleys first.

> "Strength doesn't come from what you can do.
> It comes from overcoming the things you once
> thought you couldn't." ~ Rikki Rogers

CHAPTER 2

Facing Adversity

I've offered a sneak peek into my personal history and transformation leading up to the pandemic. If you take anything from my experience, it should be this: regardless if you have a positive upbringing or one full of pain and turmoil, your future depends upon what you do now rather than where you have been. If you remain chained to your past, you will not be free to embrace the present and move into your future. A great example of this is the experience many individuals endured through the Coronavirus pandemic, me included. Today, two years since the globe shut down, many have found themselves trapped in the early days of COVID-19, traumatized by the unknowns. Initially, severely limited data showed that the number of people dying from the disease was as high as 15.5%. As science and data progressed, the actual case fatality rate of the virus was only 2% before vaccinations[1]. Unfortunately, many individuals are stuck in the past. They have accepted the fears that came with the assumption of a high death rate from the virus. Until they become open to embracing the present, including the factual data that has surfaced, they will remain chained to the past. My journey through COVID 19 was similar, where I found myself trapped in a toxic psychological state, full of fear and anxiousness for over a year. In my most vulnerable moments, I will intimately share my journey throughout the COVID 19 pandemic and how my husband and I's "rock bottom" turned into a deep drive to begin improving. I offer this narrative not to drive home the suffering that so many felt during the pandemic but instead to demonstrate how turmoil can show us what we need to improve on. Our most downtrodden days can be the windows to our higher selves. In the following chapters, I'll get into the concrete steps regarding how you can do this for yourself. Still, I hope my story serves as an excellent example to humanize the journey and demonstrate some of the concepts in action.

COVID 19 Outbreak: The Early Days

As the announcement came that our world had entered into a pandemic status, many of us were in disbelief. We were experiencing a scene from an apocalyptic movie, told that the globe was shutting down due to an unknown virus attack. As confusion and fear set into many homes, including our own, we all began to isolate, closing the doors to our friends and family. Our family's isolation was challenging as our support group primarily included those closest to us. I became incredibly overwhelmed as I was a mom raising our 2-year-old son Benson and our beautiful daughter Brooklyn, born on February 16, 2020. Bringing Brooklyn into this world brought a mixture of feelings between joy, gratitude, excitement, and love. At the same time, the pandemic coinciding with her early days on this earth created feelings of anger, scarcity, and fear for what the future may hold.

Covid 19 rattled our life and daily routines. In the beginning phases, we followed the mask mandates, sanitized everything, restricted our time in public, stopped extracurricular activities, and ultimately stopped seeing family and friends. Not just our family, everyone began to see the implications of having limited to no human connection, a vital component of a healthy life. Before COVID 19, human contact was already declining due to the significant amount of individual screen time. Research shows that a lack of human connection can be more harmful to your health than smoking, obesity, and high blood pressure[2]. Once the world began to shut down and restrictions were in place, the already problematic disconnection of our society was exasperated. The restrictions imposed by the Canadian government starting in March of 2020 included: closing and limiting non-essential businesses, eliminating and reducing different forms of social gatherings, and restricting travel and entertainment. These restrictions had different levels of severity for the following months and temporarily were removed in July of 2021 before being reimposed in September of 2021. Although the government was trying its best to protect our physical health, the constant changing of these restrictions created a yo-yo effect on people's emotions and mental health. As things started to look up and the government softened restrictions, hope became a part of our communities again. But it seemed that right when things were getting better; we were slammed with yet another round of closures and restrictions, pushing people further into anxious and depressed states. The need for freedom and connection became apparent, which only comes through unity within our society. A divided community will only create a gap in the connectivity we all thrive on.

Initial Psychological Impact on Our Family

Both my husband Kelsey and I went through different phases of mental health struggles during this time of lacking connectivity and freedom. With the onset of COVID, Kelsey found himself feeling like he was losing control of his life. As the government put restrictions in place and mandates activated, he began to think of the worst-case scenarios; for him, it was the loss of his freedom. He did not fear the virus itself but rather the loss of his ability to make decisions through his values of what made the most sense for him and his family. He was concerned with thoughts of government overreach, using the virus as a tool for authoritarian gain. These negative and consuming thoughts led to severe stress and anxiety.

Along with each negative news piece that was released, Kelsey's cognitive processes slipped further into a state of distress. As his mental health declined, it wasn't long before his physical health deteriorated. Kelsey started to experience muscle cramps and violent tremors throughout his body. These involuntary muscle spasms occurred throughout the day and were most prominent during rest. Sleep became a scarce necessity, as his body was under more stress when he slept than when he was awake. Not knowing what induced these uncontrollable tremors, Kelsey decided to seek professional help from his doctor. It became a waiting game during this season to identify what was going on as he endured multiple tests. As the hours turned into days and eventually weeks, Kelsey allowed himself to be pulled deeper into his toxic mind. He began to analyze the different possibilities of what could be happening to his body, including MS, Parkinson's, or other tremor-related diseases. His anxiety, combined with physical health concerns, led to depression. Kelsey became very withdrawn from everyday life. He lost interest in the things he found enjoyable, such as spending time with family, working out, and going for hikes and walks. His emotional state was consumed with negativity, creating a dark cloud hanging over him. I no longer recognized my husband as I once knew him.

This season we were walking through was an incredibly stressful time for our entire family. While Kelsey feared what may be happening to his body, I was worried about the worst-case scenario for me, losing my husband to a horrible disease and raising two young children on my own. I became broken internally, feeling the utmost terror I have ever experienced. As Kelsey would open up about his intimate thoughts and emotions, my fears pulled me into extreme states of sadness and despair. My heart hurt for him and the journey he was currently enduring. Through these moments, I knew that I couldn't allow myself to slip into the depressive state my husband was experiencing. I repeated to myself, "as much as you are scared right now, your husband needs you to be strong, and you need to keep the energy in the home positive for everyone. Your kids and your husband depend on you more than ever to be light in this storm." As I continued to put on a strong front, I felt so much turmoil inside. Things began to lighten for us when Kelsey received the news from his doctor that all test results came back normal. Hearing this good news brought moments of relief to our family. Kelsey's doctor asked him, "do you think it's possible that your anxiety triggered these tremors?" Leaving the doctor's office with a prescription for anxiety in hand, Kelsey became determined to find the solution to his anxiety without medication. He knew that our thoughts ingrained in our minds lead to the mental states that we experience. Kelsey reasoned that if he went to work on his internal programming, he could eradicate the anxious state he was experiencing.

As Kelsey began his growth journey, I allowed myself to let go of my "strong front" and started to slip in the opposite direction. I finally felt safe enough to let down the walls I constructed during Kelsey's health challenges. It felt like a tsunami of emotions hit me, knocking me off my feet. Countless moments of tears and sadness ensued. I remember my son Benson asking, "mommy, are you OK? What's wrong?" Soon, my despair was met with the additional fears and scarcity that I allowed to creep into my mind after our daughter was born. I became consumed with the "what ifs" and started to fear the thing I cherished the most: being a mom and raising my kids.

These fearful-driven thoughts were significant because once they were imprinted in my conscious mind and tangled with the high emotions experienced, they penetrated my subconscious mind. As Napoleon Hill describes in *Think and Grow Rich*, "your subconscious mind recognizes and acts only upon thoughts that are well mixed with emotions and feelings." These thoughts and fears overtook my subconscious thought process leading to the outcome and results that unraveled. The idea of child-rearing in a society littered with fear and discontent pushed me to feel lost, scared, and alone.

Raising our 2-year-old son during these uncertain times led to severe consequences for his developmental abilities to connect with others. He developed fears of individuals who were not a part of his immediate circle. Our son, who was once an outgoing and fearless child, now experienced fear and displeasure each time we stepped outside of our home. As we encouraged outside activities for him, I would hear Benson say things like, "oh no, mommy, there are people at the park! I don't want to go!" It was heartbreaking to see these fears take over his mind, ultimately changing his perception; what used to be a fun time was now a fearful one. Knowing in my heart that there was a need for human connectivity to live a peaceful and thriving life, I began to feel even more nervous and anxious for myself. What if our world remained in a state of disconnect and disharmony? How can my children thrive in a world such as this? It was apparent at this moment that human connection is a need to live a prosperous and fulfilled life. I began to search for this intimate connection

I desperately needed. If I can fulfill this need, I will have peace knowing my children can too.

It was almost as if Kelsey knew I was ready to find a deeper connection with something or someone. He guided me towards self-help and spiritual leader Dr. Wayne Dyer. One of the first books I picked up by Wayne was *There is a Spiritual Solution to Every Problem*. This book was incredibly inspiring, as it began to shift my perspective around experiencing moments of connection. My mind started to expand, welcoming the idea that I am connected to all things around me. I began to understand that there is an invisible and indestructible energy that flows through all of us, creating a single force field that we are all a part of. One may come to know this force field as God, Source, or Universe. Through these learnings, I experienced this unexplainable and overwhelming feeling of complete peace. Leading up to COVID-19, I had prayed for an understanding of my faith, and it was here, at this moment where it all began. I was guided towards a greater spiritual connection with God or Source and developed a knowing that we are all connected, never alone. As the well-known philosopher, Pierre Teilhard de Chardin states, I began to know that we are all spiritual beings having a human experience rather than human beings having a spiritual experience.

There is so much peace in knowing that divinity flows through every one of us and that this energy we all contain is indestructible. Although this energy of spirit is invisible to the eye, it is felt internally within our bodies, guiding us in our daily endeavors. If we slow down enough, we can open ourselves up to commune and listen to God, showing us all the solutions to our problems. I began to feel the presence of God everywhere I went; this brought warmth and comfort, knowing I was not alone. My spiritual and faith pillar began to strengthen while in the middle of this chaotic experience. Through this heightening of my faith, my psychological processes shifted back to those of a positive and enlightening nature. This adversity my family experienced through the pandemic is a profound example of how darkness can shatter the pillars of your life at any point in time if one does not continuously reinforce and elevate them. It is also essential to recognize that this darkness our family endured led to the beginning of my spiritual understanding. Before COVID 19, I was praying for a way to find my faith and become rooted in my beliefs. God answered my prayer by providing the opportunity for pain and suffering to grow through to develop my divine knowing. Without the hardships, one cannot reach the outcomes one desires. An example of this is a mom praying for patience with her children. She will receive moments of adversity that require her to build up her tolerance before she has the skill of patience. Although the psychological impact of the pandemic on my family was negative, it was the single most crucial thing that pushed me forward in my spiritual journey. I, in turn, was able to bring the positivity of my spiritual journey back to my family to help improve our collective psychological state.

State of our Nation: Mid COVID-19

In early 2021, the government announced that lifting the restrictions depended on the vaccination rates across Canada and within each province. The Canadian and United States governments paved the destructive path of disunity by announcing vaccine mandates, forcing people to choose between supporting their families and getting vaccinated. The moment the government put these requirements in place was when we saw an unhealthy level of egotism overtake our governments, countries, communities, and homes.

Additional Psychological Impact on Our Family

Pressures of inoculation and fear-mongering news created division in many of our homes, including mine. As I mentioned, some of my family feared the deadly virus while others feared the experimental vaccines. With the bombardment of conflicting information, we didn't know what was true or false. The media and influential leaders said one thing, while the doctors and experts said another. My family became severely impacted by this divide, as it deepened the existing feelings of disunity. Kelsey began to see his early fears coming into fruition; the government abusing its power to invoke control over the population, robbing individuals of their rights to make their own decisions free from coercion. He became squeezed even more now that the government had taken his actual freedoms from him.

The dark cloud that started to lift months prior rolled back in, but this time with thunder and lightning, taking out loved ones that stood in the eye of the storm. As Kelsey was making landfall in our home, I was still stuck out at sea, paddling in circles, feeling lost, unsure which way to turn. The connection I experienced with God months earlier began to fade as I allowed my cognitive process to be overwhelmed by fear. As the saying goes, faith and fear cannot coexist; it is up to you which emotion you feed, and I fed the fear. Anxieties and concerns that controlled my mind included:

- The suffocating fear of losing Kelsey to his worries and depression.
- Fear of Kelsey losing his job and the means of supporting the family.
- Concerns about how society was operating in allowing ego and negativity into our homes.

I was overwhelmed by the continued anxiousness of raising our kids in a world full of hate and anger that I no longer recognized. I slipped into a very dark place again, overcome with emotions. Our psychological struggles were paralyzing this time, as we both became stuck in our negative mental states. With both of us being down simultaneously, we fed each other's negativity. We ended up pulling each other further and further into the depths of our lower selves. Eventually, we both hit rock bottom, realizing that if we did not change the path we were on, we would sink the boats floating around us, including our kids. This realization brought tears to our eyes as we couldn't imagine a life where we allowed our thoughts to destroy all we had. At this moment, we chose to give up the need for control. A remarkable thing happened here: healing started to transpire. Through creating a safe space to connect deeply, Kelsey and I opened ourselves up to having the tough, vulnerable, and open conversations that need to happen. We talked about our psychological and emotional states and how we can begin moving from fear to faith. This key pillar of faith started the transition we unquestionably needed. Our values, family vision, and personal mission statements became our lanterns of hope through the endless blackness around us. Darkness ceased to exist as the rays of light began to emerge.

Purpose Backed by Burning Desires

This experience of realization and letting go of control was the catalyst needed to begin the next major transition Kelsey, and I would endure. Through being reconnected to our family values, we recognized the weakness in each of our foundational pillars. This realization sparked the need for change. On my end, I began to transition my focus from the depressive and anxious state our home was experiencing to the prosperous and abundant life I desired for our family. I decided to take charge of my life, and it all started with revisiting my mission statement, my purpose, which I've shared with you previously.

Bringing my purpose back into sight was the first step to activating change. My need for different results won out against the uncomfortable friction of change and evolution. This desire for more was critical as someone will only invoke change in their life if their yearnings outweigh the pain of staying the same. As you embark on your growth journey, you will notice your burning desires will grow and develop as you do. As each desire becomes fulfilled, a new one will take its place, ensuring a continuous expansion towards your higher self. Through these following chapters, we will use the COVID-19 pandemic as an example of how to grow and elevate during times of chaos. You can, however, apply the learnings from this book at any point in your life, not just through a pandemic and not just through stressful or trying times. To ignite the transformations, you desire to attain; we will first discuss the critical steps required to make changes in your life to strengthen your foundational pillars, leading towards a life of growth and fulfillment.

"With everything that has happened to you, you can either feel sorry for yourself or treat what has happened as a gift. Everything is either an opportunity to grow or an obstacle to keep you from growing. You get to choose." ~ Wayne Dyer

CHAPTER 3

Six Key Steps to Activating Lasting Change

An individual's desires can inspire change at any point in time. Whether you are living and experiencing a peaceful life or enduring a time full of turmoil, your aspirations for growth and development will shine through if they burn deeply enough. The key here is your desire for change must be strong enough to overpower your current circumstance. Once an individual's aspirations burn deeply within, the next step is to identify how one can implement the ideal transformations. Many individuals become paralyzed at this point as they are not sure how to get where they want to be, or they fundamentally do not believe it's possible. This paralysis was undoubtedly the case for Kelsey and me; our lives were like the wreckage of a sunken ship, floating in the middle of the ocean with nowhere to go. The life coaches we sought became our rescue boat, saving us from the numbing and cold water we were floating in. Their guidance pointed us in the right direction, and they exuded consistent and uplifting motivation. Their encouragement spurred our intrinsic motivation, and we began to move.

The difference between the time before COVID-19 and now is that the external circumstances were very different. Leading up to the pandemic, the ever-present darkness within society was concealed, which led to many individuals experiencing a time of prosperity and abundance. Some individuals would argue that before COVID-19, it was easier to apply personal growth and development practices because things were going well. We have never experienced the world shutting down and entering a pandemic status. At this moment, the hidden darkness within our world became magnified, leaving many individuals paralyzed and unsure of which way to go. But many also felt a pull: our lives cannot stop because of this; we must continue growing and developing personally even during the chaos. But how can one accomplish this surrounded by so much turmoil? I posit that we must apply the same key principles used before this tumultuous environment, with some additional self-assessment tools. Through guidance from others, my research, and the experience of personal transformations, I have developed a step-by-step system that I have applied to overcome the darkness that I have endured while elevating the key pillars of my life. This sequence of transformation is foundational to the success of individuals reaching their desired outcomes, regardless of the circumstances they find themselves in. I have not only applied this sequence to my own life, but I also have, over the years, coached many individuals on how to apply these steps to create lasting change in their own lives. As a result of doing the groundwork with my coaching, my clients have improved their lives significantly, and in ways, they never thought possible.

Self-development is a trendy topic today, and I don't blame you for coming into this work with preconceived notions. You may feel it's impossible to elevate yourself during a crisis. You may be skeptical of my personal story. Or you may be open and curious about the work you can do to improve yourself. Regardless of the thought space you had while entering this book; I encourage you to approach the rest of these pages with an openness and vulnerability to receiving, for you never know, there may be one thing you learn that will transform your life. Before we dive into the details, I will summarize the six critical steps that I applied to successfully activate change in my life and the change experienced by those I have coached over the years. The remaining chapters of this book will dive into the finer details, showing you how to complete each stage as you progress towards the life you desire.

6 Steps to Activating Lasting Change

1. ***Purpose Fueled by a Burning Desire***
   Identifying your purpose or vision in life can be a daunting thought for some. Your purpose will have elements of your core values woven into it. We've identified these core values through the various pillars that contribute to living a purposeful life. If you have never taken the time to discover your core values, this book will hopefully help you do so. Your pillars may differ from those I have shared, and that's precisely how it should be; we all have unique values that make up who we are. It is essential to remember your purpose can evolve and develop over time as you enter different stages of your life. Your purpose may be a compass influencing your daily decisions, always pointing you in the right direction. When and if you wander from the path you're meant to be on, your purpose, paired with a burning desire, can guide you back. Your desires or goals are the fuel needed to invoke change in your life. Once you have discovered your

greater purpose, any burning desire you have in alignment with this purpose will need to burn brightly to create the necessary persistence and determination to reach your goals. Upon revealing the truths of your values, purpose, and burning desires, I encourage you to make your own bold and unwavering mission statement if you haven't done so yet. Again, to ensure the profound impact of your declaration, be sure to include your personal pillars, purpose, and burning desires. It's OK if you're not 100% sure what your mission statement is yet; you can continue to refine it throughout your self-growth journey. As you hold onto this declaration, it will keep you pointed in the direction you intend to move.

2. *Taking Inventory*

Once you have identified your vision, it is essential to ask yourself, "am I on the right path to getting to where I want to be?" Much like when you set a GPS, you choose the final destination first, then select the path that will get you there based on where you are currently. At this step, you will learn the significance of assessing your past experiences and present moments to clarify how you got to where you are. It is imperative during this step that you take an authentic and truthful approach to your self-evaluation of these moments in time. If you fail to identify your precise location, as in where you are, you may never reach your desired destination. Again, using the GPS example, let's say you are currently in Canada, and your goal is to get to the US, but you misidentify your starting location as Thailand. Do you think setting your GPS from Thailand to the US will succeed when you are actually in Canada to start? This example shows the gravity of accurately identifying where you are beginning. In Wayne Dyer's words, "If you bring forth what is inside you, what you bring forth will save you. If you don't bring forth what is inside you, what you don't bring forth will destroy you" [1]. In other words, what you choose to accept in your past and present will bring forth clarity and a deeper understanding of how you got to where you are today. What you choose to hide from will lead to a false belief of where you are starting from, resulting in limitations in your transformation journey.

A beneficial addition to my self-assessment tools to "take inventory" throughout the Coronavirus Pandemic was utilizing Abraham Maslow's Hierarchy of Needs, also known as the different stages of growth. Maslow was an American psychologist who dedicated his time to finding the meaning of life. Through this dedication, he introduced the hierarchy of needs in 1943, which provides a framework for human advancement. These needs start from your basic needs, then move into your psychological needs, and finally into your self-fulfillment needs. This hierarchy is shown in Figure 2 and, according to Maslow, should be met in order from bottom to top. However, he concludes that there are some overlaps between the different levels of needs as individuals advance towards self-fulfillment. Additionally, each level does not require complete attainment before developing other areas; these needs can be partially met before transitioning to growth at the next stage. The key here is to remember that, for the most part, there is a requirement to have the foundational needs met before reaching the top. Much like building a house, you start with the foundation first and then build upon it your home.

Figure 2: A Rendition of Maslow's Hierarchy of Needs[2]

Using Maslow's sequence of needs will provide a framework for our self-evaluations. In addition to using this tool, you can use various other resources to deepen your assessments. In the coming chapters, I will share some of these tools with you and those I use with my clients to help them expand their evaluations. You will be well equipped to complete an in-depth review of the potential gaps present in your life, preventing you from elevating through the different stages of growth. Let's look at the three categories of needs; basic, psychological, and self-fulfilling, along with the various levels within these classifications.

Basic Needs

Our basic necessities are the lowest level of needs that require attainment before we can begin to raise upwards to our higher selves. The more fulfilled these needs are, the stronger your foundation will be to move on towards the next level of growth. These basic needs are made up of our physiological and safety needs.

> *Physiological Needs* are the basic needs foundational to ensuring our continued existence and survival. These needs include air, food, water, clothing, shelter, sex, and rest.
>
> *Safety Needs* include two components that make up an individual's overall security and include both physical and economic safety needs. Physical safety needs include the necessity of peace and freedom from war, natural disasters, violence, and illnesses. Economic safety needs are composed of financial stability, job security, and personal protection of human rights and freedoms under the law.

Psychological or Cognitive Needs

An individual's psychological needs include both social and esteem needs. As we meet our basic needs, we can shift our focus of growth to lie within our cognitive necessities, as detailed below. These levels are intricately connected to an individual's way of thinking and how our brains are wired. Later in this book, we will dive into the details of our mental programming and its importance in how we grow and develop our psychological needs. For now, let's take a look at the specifics of these two levels of growth.

Social Needs are the first level of our cognitive needs and start with the necessity of belonging and love. Humans have an emotional need to feel a sense of belonging, connectedness, and love through friendships, relationships, social groups, community groups, and faith groups. Harvard researcher Shawn Achor shares that social connection is as impactful on the longevity of life as smoking, high blood pressure, and obesity. How we view our relationships holds significant consequences, and these views directly result from our own thought processes.

Esteem Needs encompass two parts and include our lower esteem and higher esteem. An individual's lower esteem is made up of the need for acknowledgment, respect, and appreciation from others—external sources of validation support this form of esteem. The wiring of our minds highly influences the perception of these validations. What one individual sees as acceptance, another may see as rejection. In addition to outside approval, each individual also requires internal acceptance. This internal validation is called higher esteem and is made of self-respect, self-worth, self-confidence, and independence. As you can see, both levels of esteem needs are made up of our cognitive thoughts, resultantly impacting the fulfillment of these needs. You will learn a great deal more about the mind and how we can control our thought processes to ensure the satisfaction of our esteem needs throughout the rest of this book.

Self-Fulfillment Needs

Self-fulfillment is the highest level of motivation where an individual's drive to satisfy their needs is at its peak. Approaching this level, you have fulfilled some, if not most, of your basic and psychological necessities. According to Maslow, self-fulfillment is composed of one level of growth, self-actualization.

> *Self-Actualization* is a state in which an individual pursues growth and development, working towards their ideal self. At this level, you are focused on achieving gratification and purpose in your life. Here, you are free from prejudice and unhealthy levels of egotism while fostering creativity and higher awareness. If one desires to remain at this level of advancement, there must be a solid foundation within their lower needs. If the basic and psychological needs crumble, so will the self-fulfillment needs.

Taking an inventory of where you are at with each of these levels of needs will be critical in identifying where you need to start with your personal growth journey. I will emphasize the need for ultra-transparency again with yourself on potential requirements that may be missing in your hierarchy, holding you back from achieving your full potential in life. Don't worry if you feel unequipped to take this inventory; we will dive into this at length later on, and I will walk you through it step by step.

3. ***Take Ownership***
   After completing an inventory assessment of where you are at, including a review of your past and present, the next step is to begin the process of *Taking Ownership*. It is consequential to accept full responsibility for your thoughts, emotions, reactions, and choices as they have led to today's results. There is no room for blame on the journey towards living a self-fulfilled and abundant life. You will only be given what you can handle, which comes with great accountability. For someone to exude these responsible and accountable characteristics, they

must first accept ownership of their life. A significant part of taking responsibility is assessing the nature of your intrinsic mindset within your thinking processes. The natural sway of your internal processing can bend towards a closed and fixed mindset, or it can lean towards an open and growth mindset. A closed mind is rigid in its beliefs and capabilities, meaning the individual does not believe in evolution or development. Since they see their traits as fixed, these individuals tend to blame or even lie about their circumstances. They do not want to be seen as a failure when faced with adversity. They tie the outcomes in life to their self-worth as an individual.

In contrast, those with an open, growth mindset do not see adversity as a failure but as a learning opportunity. They do not believe their capabilities are fixed or limited; therefore, they do not misidentify their self-worth as connected to their outcomes. This limitless disposition creates an environment that fosters accountability and ownership.

In the coming chapters, you will learn how to complete a self-assessment of the nature of your internal processes. This evaluation can reveal the roots of an individual's lack of ownership in life if it exists. You will gain clarity around the detrimental outcome if you choose to remain in a state of blame for your past and present. It will become apparent that how you live one area of your life reflects how you live all areas of your life. You can either continue down the path of blame, leaving the outcomes of your life in others' hands, or step up, take responsibility, and put your life back into your own hands. You, and no one else, are responsible for where you are today. Once you can accept this, you will unlock the power of being able to own your future.

4. ***Create a Plan and Take Action***

Now that you know exactly where you want to be, where you are currently at and have accepted full responsibility, it is now time to develop a plan and take action to move in the direction of your desired outcome. Remember, because you have accepted responsibility for your past and present, you can now be accountable for your future as YOU are responsible for your own actions. This accountability is a requirement as you create an action plan because you are the one who will be implementing these positive changes towards growth. Creating a plan that will genuinely activate change will take time. You must consider all critical points of interest, including; your values, starting location, the direction of progression, and potential obstacles on your way to your desired outcomes. For example, as you evaluate your values, it is paramount that your plan aligns with these values. Otherwise, you will feel like you are going in the wrong direction.

Consider the following scenario: you are evaluating ways to expand your family income, and you are offered a new job that requires a significant amount of travel out of town. If one of your values is time with your family, but the plan you are considering requires you to leave your loved ones, even if it is otherwise a good opportunity, then it may be worth re-evaluating this plan. A part of this re-evaluation is identifying potential solutions that can ensure your alignment with your family pillar. This scenario is only one example of the many decisions we face daily. Each choice you make is either contributing to your plan or hindering it; this is why establishing and applying your personal value system is essential. As you continue to explore the following pages, you will learn how to create a plan geared towards setting up the conditions for inevitable success. We will apply a transformative framework that I use in my coaching business to help individuals develop goals that are actionable on a deep level. Your plan will lead you towards self-fulfillment when designing your strategy by applying this system.

5. ***Overcoming Obstacles***

As you embark on the journey of putting your plan into action to create change, it is vital to consider the potential roadblocks one may face. The transformation journey can be compared to the adventure of climbing to the peak of a mountain. The higher you climb, the more wind and tumultuous weather you may experience. Similarly, as you climb towards your higher self, more obstacles will be present as you elevate in your growth journey. You may endure external challenges from friends and family who disapprove or don't understand the journey you are pursuing. Your decisions to rise and elevate can create waves in the bay, causing the surrounding boats to rock. Those around you may fall into these two categories as you evolve and change: They are not used to the rocking motion or the positivity and growth you are exuding, so they will cause friction. Your new higher vibration no longer aligns with their low vibrations, and they are fearful of it and don't understand it. On the other hand, some may be excited to see and share your journey and will join in with you. It's essential to note these moments as they will reveal who is on your side cheering you on or who is the anchor to your boat. And remember, any objections, judgments, or criticisms expressed by others are not a personal attack on you; it is their own fear looking for ways to be expressed.

In addition to the external challenges you may face, you may also encounter internal obstacles that can be severely destructive to your growth journey. These obstructions are personal character traits: procrastination, lack of persistence, fear of failure, approval-seeking, and dependency. These characteristics may feel like an anchor holding you back from taking the desired steps forward. Understanding the many components of these qualities can help you diagnose the blind spots hindering your progression. I will detail these potential obstructions in the coming chapters of this book and how to work through each one of them.

6. ***Review & Assess***
   As you courageously take action in your life, it is paramount that you understand the difference between progressive action and regressive action. Just because you are making changes does not guarantee that you will be moving closer to your goals. Let's consider an individual who wants to live a healthier lifestyle to increase their energy levels. The first habit they decide to change is to quit smoking cigarettes. They have decided to implement new practices in place of their old ones along their transformation journey to make the change sustainable. Still, many may forget to consider that their new habits may not be in alignment with their desired outcome. It is crucial to ask yourself what these changes are and the action that accompanies them; are they progressive or regressive? Will my new habits contribute to my goals or hinder them? Going back to the individual who has decided to quit smoking, they have decided that their new habit involves snacking on food to keep their minds preoccupied. If they go down the route of consuming junk food, chocolate, and potato chips, they may see success in quitting the smoking habit, but now they are creating another toxic habit of unhealthy eating. They have replaced one bad habit with another, still contributing to the original exhaustion problem. This choice is what I call

a regressive habit change, where the new habit is just as toxic, if not worse. Alternatively, let's say the individual chooses to consume fruits and vegetables in place of their smoking habit. Yes, it is still food; however, it is full of nutrition that provides the body with energy. They will see success in eliminating the unhealthy habit of smoking, and they will also boost their energy levels by providing their body with the nutrients it needs. This choice is a simple example of progressive habit change, where the individual is moving towards their desired goal, health, and energy. In addition to assessing the nature of your actions, whether they are progressive or regressive, it is also paramount to be reviewing the following consistently:

- Are the original goals you have set the aspirations you desire to continue working towards? As you elevate and reach critical milestones throughout your transformation journey, your desires may evolve and change. As you grow, so too will your vision.
- While you pursue living your best life, you might become distracted by your surroundings and circumstances. It is invaluable and non-negotiable to regularly "check in" with yourself. These mini self-assessments will ensure you maintain your alignment with your values and the direction you wish to move in.
- Although you may have selected a plan or a road map to guide you towards self-fulfillment, it is essential to examine your chosen plan regularly. Is this path still the ideal and right path for me to continue down? There can be many different roads between your starting point and your destination.

Summary

Utilizing these six pivotal steps to change can have a profound impact on the direction of an individual's journey in life and can be applied at any point in time. Yes, chaotic times can radically alter someone's path they had laid out for themselves, which happened for many individuals when COVID-19 transpired. The critical thing to remember is that it's not about staying on the path 100% of the time but rather about finding your way back when you venture off the course. I hope that the six steps to change can help you with a roadmap as you embark on your own growth journey, bringing abundance and peace into your home.

We've discussed the importance of establishing your *Purpose Fueled by a Burning Desire* on our journey so far. After this first phase of elevation is Step 2, *Taking Inventory* of your past and present to identify the areas of growth desired. To guide you through this self-assessment process, I will continuously use the COVID 19 pandemic as an example throughout our journey. I will dig into the events that unfolded and the different influences on our nation's viewpoints that exacerbated the fright, confusion, anger, and separation felt throughout. These outcomes had a significant impact on all levels of our hierarchy of needs, which I will take the time to unpack with you. To be clear, this book is not only applicable to COVID-19 times but also an apt example of a challenging and turbulent time that we can use to convey the journey toward self-actualization. As you approach the rest of our time together, I encourage you to empty yourself of ego, releasing judgments, criticisms, and comparisons. Bringing empathy and understanding will help you jump into the minds of others, recognizing that we are all unique in our ways, including our beliefs and thoughts. Understanding the many environmental influences on individuals' choices and actions helped me accept the differences and uniqueness in our situations. I hope these next few chapters will do the same for you and bring clarity around how to complete these detailed evaluations for yourself.

"Take inventory of yourself, see if any remnants of fear are standing in your way. Then you may grow... Because nothing, absolutely nothing, can stand in your way" ~Napoleon Hill

CHAPTER 4

Taking Inventory: Psychological Processes

The traumatic events many of us encounter, including collective traumas like the Coronavirus Pandemic, can leave a lasting impression of anxiety and numbness. As paralyzed and frightened many individuals feel throughout their day-to-day activities, it is paramount that we begin to move. Only then can we bring warmth and feeling back into our numb bodies. This 6-Step process of activating change in our lives is the key to thawing out our frozen states. So far, you have been enlightened to the first step of identifying your values and *Purpose Fueled by a Burning Desire*. The second is to take an inventory of your past and present moments to acquire the knowledge needed to understand where you are. We will continue in this chapter with Step 2, *Taking an Inventory*, as we further expand our evaluations. Up to this point, we have covered the early and progressive stages of the pandemic, taking note of the external circumstances, actions, and results that have ensued. Throughout this chapter, we will look at the internal impacts as we dive into understanding the psychological processes that we all engage in. Although everyone has the existence of a thought sequence, each individual has unique components making up these processes. You will learn more about how our beliefs and thoughts lead to the outcomes we experience with each situation.

Beliefs

Understanding the events and developments in your past and present is only the first step when taking an inventory. It is just as critical to understanding your inner programming when taking in the information provided by these events or happenings. This internal processing is composed of two components that influence the operation of our minds and includes the conscious mind and the subconscious mind. The conscious mind is the part of our psychological process that we are aware of and consists of our thoughts, stimulations, perceptions, memories, and desires. This awareness allows for observations, contemplation, and decision-making to occur. The subconscious mind is that part of our processing that is automatic, requiring no thought. This part of the mind is also known as our habitual mind and is responsible for bodily functions, storing imprinted thoughts, emotions, values, doctrines, and beliefs. This subconscious programming guides us through everyday life and is responsible for how we perceive things. The way an individual sees one thing may differ from how others perceive that same thing. This variability in our perceptions is due to the unique habitual mind that we all have. Since our stored thought processes are made up of our ideas and beliefs, we must understand what forms these internal truths we all have. A belief is something that we see as the truth and is developed through our personal experiences or through adopting the ideas of others. Throughout our younger impressionable years, these ideologies or ways of thinking within our subconscious minds are established as children. As a child, these experiences have a significant impact on the biology and makeup of the brain, ultimately impacting your mental, physical and social health. Since beliefs are relative to how we see the world around us, one can conclude that our views will change as our perceptions and programming change.

Let's look at how an individual's programming alters how they perceive an experience or event. Consider a scenario where two individuals are evaluating an opportunity to snorkel at the Great Barrier Reef. The first individual, as a child, indulged in watching movies and TV shows involving terrorizing shark attacks. From these experiences, they have developed a thought process that assumes all sharks are dangerous and are at significant risk of encountering hazardous sharks if they complete this experience. From this mental complex, the individual has formed a fear of sharks. This fear will impact their choice when deciding to swim the Great Barrier Reef. Now, if you ask the second individual, a marine biologist specializing in the study of sharks, they will tell you something very different. Since their thoughts are developed around understanding the behaviors and characteristics of sharks, they will tell you that not all sharks are dangerous. Roughly 12 out of approximately 300 different species of sharks are known to be involved in human shark attacks.[1] Other statistics can shed some light on the risks of a shark attack compared to other life-threatening situations. For example, there are roughly 12 deaths from shark attacks each year, in comparison to approximately 360,000 deaths from drowning[2]. This abundance of knowledge leads the individual to experience feelings of excitement when provided the opportunity to experience the Great Barrier Reef. This simple example shows that our environmental influences and ignorance of the facts regarding any subject or event will skew our perceptions of how we see the world around us. We may only have a small piece of information, providing a fraction of the picture rather than the whole canvas. Our minds operate under the assumption that what we see and perceive is fact and is the truth. It is imperative to understand that our personal realities become constructed from our experiences and influences, so each person's "truth" may differ. So how do we distinguish our personal truths from the actual truth? The answer to this question lies in understanding the belief cycle. Let's look at the Belief Cycle in Figure 3 and its role in each of our minds.

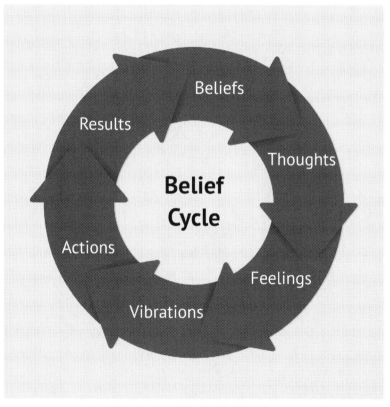

Figure 3: The Belief Cycle

Thoughts

In addition to knowing the significance of our beliefs and how they determine the perceptions of our environment, we must also understand the influential role these beliefs play in the outcomes we encounter, as shown in Figure 3. Knowing this connection is paramount in determining how one can alter the results of their life. Based on this cognitive process, you can conclude that you will change the outcomes of your life if you change your beliefs. Now let's dive into how we can begin the process of altering our programmed minds to elevate towards our best selves.

When there is a stimulus from our external environment, taken in by one of the five senses, this stimulus creates a thought that first enters our conscious mind. As you have learned, our conscious mind is composed of our desires, memories, and thoughts. Here, our minds are constantly evolving, and where we utilize our imagination, creativity, and problem-solving. These thoughts that enter our conscious minds are full of energy, vibrating at different frequencies. Once they have penetrated our brains, they trigger a release of certain chemicals throughout the body, leading to the feelings experienced. These feelings are then relayed back to the brain, further enhancing our original thoughts and releasing more of the same chemicals. The individual then has entered into a chemically driven loop between our thoughts and feelings.

If an individual has an adverse event or stimulus picked up by one or more of the five senses, this will trigger lower energy thoughts and emotions, such as stress. A stress response chemically signals the body to enter into a "fight or flight" mode. According to neurology expert Dr. Joe Dispenza, this activation of the stress response creates a momentary boost in energy that can create an addictive experience. This addiction can lead individuals to become attached to their problems, hostile environments, unfortunate outcomes, and toxic relationships as they thrive off of the brief energy high experienced.[3]

Many individuals do not know that we have a choice to allow these thoughts and chemicals released to continue to have their corresponding effect on the body, or they can choose to alter them as they desire. If we allow the thought-emotion loop to continue, these thoughts and feelings will imprint into our subconscious mind, where they will either support existing beliefs or create a new one. It is here where they will be filed and stored for future use. Although we have control of these thoughts that become imprinted in our subconscious minds, once a habitual thought does become stored, it is more challenging to change, unlike those thoughts that come and go in the conscious mind. In Napoleon Hill's book, *Think and Grow Rich*, he wrote that "we have control of what enters our subconscious mind, but not everyone exercises this control."[4] The question becomes how do we exercise this control over our subconscious mind?

As Napoleon Hill suggests, we can use the concept of autosuggestion, where we intentionally imprint our minds with the words and thoughts that will alter the chemicals released, ultimately changing our stored beliefs. This process of imprinting our minds involves a four-step process:

1. Developing an awareness of our thoughts.
2. Having a desire and willingness to change these thoughts.
3. Creating new empowering thought.
4. Downloading these new thoughts into our neural network through autosuggestion.

It is not as simple as it sounds, though; rewiring our brains to think differently requires breaking our old ways of perceiving the world and being open to receiving new information that may go against our psychological complexes. As individuals become aware of and evaluate their current beliefs, thoughts, and emotions, they shift from an unconscious state of being to one that is consciously aware. This awareness prevents the accidental acceptance of undesirable beliefs, thoughts, and emotions. Establishing consciousness leads to a state of curiosity, inquisitiveness, and openness to learning. As an individual's knowledge expands, so will the neural networks wired into our brains, making it easier to alter our subconscious thoughts. By knowing the desired outcomes that you would like to achieve, you will be able to identify the new ideas and feelings that you must install. Your commitment to mentally repeat and review this desired self, including the new thoughts and emotions that must accompany this desired state, will lead to the fundamental neurological transformation of the mind.

Suppose someone is genuinely open to taking in new knowledge and altering their old ways of thinking to include newfound wisdom. In that case, they may encounter uncomfortable feelings of change. The process of transforming our thoughts is a habit change on its own. Individuals must recognize that breaking a bad habit and replacing it with a good one takes time. One of today's top life and business coaches, Tony Robbins, shares that it takes about three to four weeks of intentionality to change your mindset.[5] For example, think of a time in your life when you desired to quit a bad habit, such as eliminating sugar, quitting smoking, or eliminating alcohol. It most likely took you time to stop the cravings, where you could go on about your day without even thinking about the harmful habit. In addition to eliminating the bad habit, you are also implementing a positive routine to replace the bad one. Let's say you desire to quit eating sugar; to accomplish this effectively, we must replace this with something healthy, such as having a glass of water or eating a piece of fruit or vegetables. The key here is to take time to study yourself to identify what positive habits can help you overcome the negative patterns.

Developing an awareness of our thoughts and identifying the

ones we would like to change is the first step in this transformation process. Next is implementing the method of autosuggestion by implanting new ideas into your brain through affirmations, reading, podcasts, visualization, and other positive, thought-provoking, and stimulating activities. Activating this process occurs when new neural patterns are established in the brain while releasing new chemicals to induce new emotions. You have now entered into a new thought-emotion loop.

Thinking back to the example of swimming with sharks, the naive individual who regularly watches videos on shark attacks had a stimulus from the outside world, in this case, videos, impacting the senses of sight and hearing. This stimulus from the environment enters the mind, leading to the development of thought, creating their personal truth. In this case, the individual with no or limited experience with sharks will likely perceive all sharks as bad. If this is the truth accepted, then the brain will trigger the release of certain chemicals to induce the feelings within the body that go along with this negative thought. Resultantly, the individual will experience negative emotions. We can change and reinforce better neural pathways in our minds by altering our habits, eventually creating a new "truth."

Emotions or Feelings

The emotions or feelings we experience resulting from specific thoughts that enter our conscious minds play an essential role in whether or not these thoughts become stored for future use. We must recognize it is not enough to have words or stimulants replayed in our brains to begin the process of rewiring; we must also combine them with feelings and emotions to have a lasting impact, as shown in Figure 3. Emotions can be intentionally altered by integrating new knowledge into our thinking processes and visually seeing new and desired experiences. This visualization will trigger the release of new chemicals leading to the formation of new emotions. It is imperative that you also understand that not all emotions have the same impact. Each feeling has a specific frequency or vibrational energy due to the chemical signature that induces these emotions. The difference between positive and negative emotions is that negative emotions operate at lower frequencies, having an energy-draining effect on the body. These lower energy emotions will voluntarily combine with thoughts ensuring they imprint on the subconscious mind. Positive emotions operate at a higher frequency, bringing an abundance of energy into the body. To ensure the imprint of these positive emotions, an individual must apply conscious effort through autosuggestion to have a lasting impact on our subconscious minds. This intentionality requires more work over the natural imprint of negative emotions. In addition to the distinctions between the two types of emotions, negative and positive, each category also has uniqueness. There are what we call major emotions, negative or positive, that have a more significant impact on our subconscious or habitual minds. For example, consider the major negative emotion of extreme fear. These feelings will have a significantly lower frequency than other minor negative emotions such as doubtfulness. In this case, the lower the frequency, the more significantly our minds are negatively impacted. Positive emotions are the opposite, where the higher the frequency of emotions, the more significant the positive impact will be.

Since positive and negative emotions cannot coexist, we must be diligent in our intentionality of ensuring positive emotions dominate our minds. Again, this can be accomplished through awareness of our thinking patterns, adding knowledge to expand our neural networks, and visually seeing the outcomes we desire. This combination of actions will trigger new and positive emotions leading to your ideal life.

From Napoleon's research, he has identified the major emotions in Table 1 that have the most significant impact on our vibrations and their lasting impressions. I share these major emotions or feelings here so you can take notice of the negative and lower energy ones and purposefully go to work on replacing them with the ideal positive emotions.

Table 1: Major Positive and Negative Emotions[4]

Major Positive Emotions	Major Negative Emotions
Desire	Fear
Faith	Jealousy
Love	Hatred
Sex	Revenge
Enthusiasm	Greed
Romance	Superstition
Hope	Anger

Reviewing the shark example again, if the individual experiences a negative emotion of fear due to the stimulus and thoughts experienced, over time, the narrative that all sharks are dangerous will become a consistent or habitual cognitive process that will implant into their subconscious mind. If, however, the individual experiences no emotions at all, then the thought can be stored with limited impact on the individual, or it can simply be pushed aside, moving on to the next thought.

Vibrations

It is shown in Figure 3 that once we have a thought and combine it with feelings, we determine the level of vibration. As you learned already, another way of looking at vibrations is the frequency of each emotion. Positive thoughts will yield higher vibrations, whereas negative thoughts will produce lower vibrations. "Thought impulses begin immediately to translate themselves into their physical equivalent whether those thoughts are voluntary or involuntary."[4] This implies that the negative or positive energies that we allow to vibrate within our minds will result in the physical form of having higher or lower energies. For example, fearful thoughts combined with emotions of fear create lower energy vibrations as experienced by the individual who has developed a fear of sharks. Those who operate and engage in lower energy vibrations will notice energy drains or leaks within their life, leading to the experience of tiredness, laziness, lack of motivation, and exhaustion. In contrast, faithful thoughts combined with the emotions of faith create higher energy vibrations. These individuals will experience higher energy levels leading to a spirited nature, feeling energized, motivated, and rested.

Actions & Results

Now that we understand the impact our thoughts and emotions have on our vibrations, we can look at how our actions and outcomes are derived. Higher frequency thoughts and vibrations will foster a problem-solving environment invoking intuition, insight, and inspiration. This environment will positively influence our actions ensuring alignment with the nature of our vibrations, ultimately leading to desirable results. Again, let's look at faithful thoughts paired up with the emotions of faith, creating higher frequency vibrations. This thought process will lead to actions of having faith in oneself, faith in others, and faith in that which is greater. The outcome of these actions can only be positive since they are derived from higher frequency energies. Now let's look at negative thoughts on the opposite end of the spectrum. Lower frequency thoughts will induce the environments of skepticism, doubt, and ego. These lower energy environments will generate negative actions resulting in undesirable outcomes. Let's consider the negative thought process of doubt. The reduced frequency of vibrations created by these thoughts and emotions will manifest actions of disbelief in oneself and others. These actions can only lead to a negative outcome, as that is the disposition of these thoughts.

Going back to swimming the Great Barrier Reef, the individual with negative thoughts and emotions regarding sharks will result in lower energy vibrations. The results must be in alignment with that of a negative nature. The individual who experiences paralysis from fear will likely make decisions based on these emotions, missing out on experiencing one of the world's seven natural wonders. However, if this individual desires to alter this thought process, they must start with authentically identifying their inner beliefs and negative thoughts and emotions. Next, they must begin the process of autosuggestion, where they become open to the journey of discovery along with the process of change. As the individual expands their knowledge, their open spirit will allow them to compare their stored beliefs with the new information, creating new neural pathways. Here the individual now has a choice to alter their inner truths to encompass any further information they become enlightened with. Suppose the individual afraid of sharks chooses to educate themselves regarding the risks associated with sharks and swimming in the ocean. In that case, they will have an opportunity to transform their inner beliefs completely. By changing their thoughts and emotions, over time with diligent effort, the individual's new truths will be those made up of facts with a positive nature rather than the negative and naive thoughts initially created.

To take full advantage of the principles we have discussed, you must complete your self-evaluation, being as open and authentic as possible with acknowledging your personal beliefs, thoughts, and emotions. Only then can you truly know where you reside with your inner world. Here you must ask yourself, are you genuinely open to receiving new factual information, or are you closed off to the opportunity for enrichment? Once you uncover the level of your openness to enlightenment, you will reveal the amount of growth available to you. If we desire to create positive results, we must be diligent in monitoring our beliefs and controlling our thoughts. Wayne Dyer's words summarize this idea perfectly: "as you think, so shall you be ." Now that we understand that we are the masters of our minds let's look at the psychological outcomes and the fears that have transpired through the COVID-19 pandemic as an example of how many individuals allowed fears to take root. Here, you have an opportunity to use this experience to learn from and apply this gained knowledge at any point in your life. As you continue to read, I encourage you to consider how this information may apply to other experiences you have endured.

Thoughts and Emotions Experienced During COVID-19

It is essential to take the time to appreciate and understand that we all share different fears and outcomes based on our unique beliefs, thoughts, and journeys in life, including through the COVID-19 pandemic. As you have read earlier in this chapter, our beliefs and thoughts are the prerequisites to our outcomes, placing the sole responsibility of our lives into our own hands. Applying the learnings from this chapter, let's dig into the different individual beliefs, thoughts, and fears due to the pandemic events. Because beliefs and thoughts are an internal process for each individual, I will begin my analysis at the stage of emotions because they are external and measurable. Keep in mind that an individual's emotions are indicators of their thoughts and beliefs, so once you understand their emotions, you can develop some understanding of their beliefs.

As I share the different concerns people are experiencing, I encourage all readers to keep an open and soft heart for individuals' various psychological journeys, even if you do not share them. There are no right or wrong feelings. Reading these words with a willingness to be open to receiving and empathizing with each of our intimate thoughts is the first step to growing our mental health and connectivity in our communities. As Wayne Dyer says, "The measure of mental health is the disposition to find good everywhere." In other words, the more we choose positive thoughts, searching for the good, the healthier our psychological health will be.

Four Main Fears

The physiological condition of our society has taken a significant turn for the worse during COVID 19. Different fears plagued our globe at various stages of the pandemic. This anguish could be categorized into four main categories of fear, as determined by Irvin D Yalom, a well-known psychiatrist. He categorized fear into the following "ultimate concerns of life": death, freedom, isolation, and meaninglessness.[6] It is essential to mention that these main concerns also contain numerous sub concerns. As you learn about these common fears, recognize that they existed before COVID 19, and they will continue to be a part of humanity as we move past this time. To reiterate, the unfortunate events of the pandemic led to the magnification of the turmoil that already existed. This visibility led our society's collective to experience the toxicity that already existed, but it brought extreme awareness of its presence. For this reason, I will continue to use this case study to highlight what many of us now know to be true. Let's review the four main fears that plague many individuals' lives, both during and outside the pandemic.

Death

The fear of death is also considered the fear of loss. Just the idea of leaving this world with nothing and alone is enough to trigger anxieties. Not knowing when the end may come or what happens afterlife is frightful for some, especially if there is a need to understand and control everything. Other sub fears include illness, injury & pain.

Freedom

Yalom considered this to be a fear of having too much freedom. The responsibility for one's actions, feelings, deficiencies, and discomforts resides solely on the individual and can create an overwhelming feeling that induces fears and anxieties. You can also look at the fear of freedom as the dread of the possibility of losing your autonomy. Without your ability of personal expression, you fear losing your uniqueness. Losing our free will can also be viewed as trapped, captive, powerless, and controlled (losing control).

Isolation

The fear of isolation is also considered the fear of loneliness, which can occur in present moments as you are physically alone. It can be a fear of solitude happening in the future. Humanity is designed with the need for connection and a sense of belonging, especially in uncertain and trying times. Isolation can be very uncomfortable for some as it can lead to one's vulnerability when left alone with only their thoughts. Other fears encompassed in this main concern include losing someone, losing love, losing support, fear of judgment, fear of rejection, and fear of being alone.

Meaninglessness

Meaninglessness is when someone or something has no significance or meaning. In Yalom's words, "humans are meaning-seeking creatures in a world without a universal sense of meaning."[6] This can create significant confusion as individuals embark on a journey to find meaning and purpose in their lives. Other fears that are part of meaninglessness include:

- Lack of purpose.
- Having no direction.
- Being unnoticed.
- Being unappreciated.
- Lack of impact.
- The fear of changing directions.

Summary

As you have learned earlier, fear is a negative emotion and can only yield negative actions and outcomes. The result of these negative dispositions includes judgment, criticism, anger, frustration, and hate. We can see clearly that these emotions are expressed by the many leaders and influencers of our nations. Finger-pointing, accusations, division, manipulation, and blame have become the norm among the leaders of our society, which then penetrates the citizens of our communities. This result of this toxicity led to a 273% jump in mental health concerns with the onset of the Coronavirus pandemic. The Household Pulse Survey completed by the U.S Census Bureau reported that 41.1% of adults reported symptoms of anxiety and depression in the early months[7]. Whether you are experiencing psychological wrath from the pandemic or evaluating your mental health outside of this time, you must thoroughly assess your own cognitive state.

Individuals must consider the impacts of their emotions and the potential trigger of our stress responses. If you recall earlier in this chapter, experiencing the 'flight or fight' reaction from stress and other mental health concerns can lead to addictive highs from this mental state. You must ask yourself if you are keeping yourself trapped in these lower energy thoughts and emotions because of your addiction to them. Our awareness and willingness to rewire our thinking patterns are essential to begin the process of healing, which then opens up our lives to abundance and possibility. Additionally, we all must start to recognize and accept that our narratives, beliefs, and values may be different from one another, and that is OK. If this concept sounds large and intimidating now, don't worry, we will dive into rewiring our thinking patterns and accept our differences later in our journey.

> "It is not our differences that divide us. It is our inability to recognize, accept, and celebrate those differences." ~ Audre Lorde

CHAPTER 5

Take Inventory: Major Influences on Our Beliefs

By understanding the belief cycle and how it shapes our realities, we can begin the exciting journey of designing the life we desire. Imagine you have a magic wand capable of granting yourself three wishes; what would those wishes be? Write them down. Now, envision you are told that a box will hold these three burning desires and will only be released as your inner being elevates into the person necessary for that wish to come to fruition. Let's look at the typical outcome of broke or highly in debt individuals who win the lottery to humanize this metaphor. Those who have trouble managing their money before any financial winnings have the ingrained beliefs that go along with poor money management. Remember, our beliefs shape our outcomes. Therefore, if the broke and debt-ridden individual wins a million dollars and they do not change their beliefs and habits around financial management, they will find themselves back to where they started, if not worse.

The same is true about your desires for more. You will only be given what you can handle, and if you are given too much, it will be taken away. This outcome shows the gravity of altering our inner being, consisting of our beliefs, thoughts, and emotions to align with our desired results. As you have learned in the last chapter, the process of autosuggestion is how we can alter and grow our stored beliefs to match the outcomes we desire. This inner transformation requires being open to changing our views through discovery and action. In addition to transforming our psychological processes, there is another significant component we must understand to reach our aspirations. This chapter will look at the major influences on our beliefs, apart from the early years of programming. Since our beliefs are a function of thoughts and emotions, these major influences will be those that impact our thought and emotion loops. As individuals understand these potential impacts on their cognitive and emotional complexes, they will be well equipped to create an environment fertile for growth, change, and elevation of their beliefs. There are four components that I will cover that impact our internal programming, which alters the outcomes we experience in life. These four influences on our beliefs include Inner Dialogue, Stimulus & Energy Levels, Self-Esteem & Egotism, and Ignorance & Knowledge. This chapter will demonstrate how these components are deeply connected to individuals' beliefs. We will begin taking an inventory of these four impacts by first acknowledging whether they are present, and then we will start to assess each component. It is important to note that these assessments will be expanded upon in the following chapters using a coaching sequence geared towards deepening self-evaluations. For now, we will approach this chapter with a high-level review of these four elements, which will be the foundation for the expanded evaluations completed later.

Inner Dialogue

An individual's inner dialogue is the intimate self-speech that we partake in within our minds and is very different from the momentary thoughts that come and go. Our internal communications are conversions we engage in with ourselves and reflect our inner world. They will have a nature that matches our programming and may have a positive or negative disposition. Our internal dialogue serves as a way to validate or support our deeply rooted beliefs. The moment we challenge our self-speech, we are consequently challenging our beliefs. The uncomfortable feelings you experience when your mental dialogue does not match your beliefs confirm this connection. For example, suppose you have a deeply rooted belief that you should engage in regular physical activity to stay healthy. You notice your internal dialogue, trying to convince yourself that it would be better to stay in your pajamas and watch TV. In that case, you will experience uncomfortable feelings of guilt and irritability. These emotions will arise because your self-speech does not align with your ingrained beliefs. Understanding that our beliefs and internal conversations are connected, we can conclude that if we change our inner dialogue, we can create an environment that supports the alteration of our beliefs. As you elevate and engage in positive and encouraging self-talk, you will begin to contribute to the changes in your belief system that you desire. Using Napoleon Hill's teachings, we unraveled the ability of all individuals to control their thoughts through the process of autosuggestion. So, what does this process look like, and how can we apply it to our intimate self-talk? Autosuggestion is when someone controls the stimulus that reaches the subconscious mind through the five senses: taste, touch, sight, hearing, and smell. Once you have identified the dominating negative thoughts and feelings and desire to change them, you can lean on the five senses to accomplish this. Let's look at the acknowledgments and assessments you can consider to help take an inventory of your internal dialogue.

Acknowledge: First, you must recognize if there is the presence of these lower energy thoughts and the level of impact they have on your everyday life. By consciously tuning into your inner dialogue, you will elevate your awareness, which is the first step toward identifying the negative, low-energy thoughts. I encourage you to make a list or take note of this inner dialogue. If you recognize these negative thoughts controlling or impacting your outcomes, you must move on to the next step, assessment. Here, you will learn about the in-depth review needed to start rewiring your mindset to encompass positive and uplifting thoughts.

Assessment: Here, you will identify the roots of your negative and lower energy thoughts and emotions. Let's look at two of the five senses, sight and hearing, and how they can be the triggers for these lower energy thoughts. Sight, of course, is how we take in visual information and has a profound impact on how we perceive and remember things. These perceptions can be positive or negative. Hearing is the sense that picks up sound from our external environments and plays a significant role in how events and outcomes are stored subconsciously. Combining these two senses is critical to understanding the entirety of our environments. Our minds utilize our senses in combination with one another to take in the full experiences of our world. Let's look at the most common environmental inputs that use these senses: social media, news, ads, associations, books, podcasts, videos, TV, and movies. Take note of each input that involves complaining, judgments, comparisons, anger, violence, fear, hate, scarcity, and any other lower energy expression. Any time one of these environmental inputs causes you to experience negative thoughts and emotions, you have identified a root cause for your unhealthy self-speech. To remedy this, you can deliberate about the input you allow yourself to receive. Curate the content that you take in, in large part, so that it creates positive vibrations in your inner dialogue.

Stimulus & Energy Levels

Additional factors that impact our mental processes are the many different stimulants or energies created by our environments and the activities we partake in. Through my extensive learning and coaching experiences, I have learned a lot about the many factors influencing one's energy levels. I can summarize these factors into three energy zones, including the Cognitive Zone, Physical Zone, and Environmental Zones. All three of these zones contain energies that contribute to an individual's overall or total energy level. By ensuring our energy zones are operating at peak levels, we will create an evolutionary environment and ensure that we have the fuel needed to engage in rewiring our brains. Let's dig into these three energy zones to understand how they play a role in our overall energy levels.

Cognitive Energy Zone

This energy zone is a limitless energy field encompassing our thoughts, beliefs, and values. We have two contributors to the energy experienced within this zone: our conscious and subconscious thinking processes. You have discovered earlier in this book that our conscious thoughts are those that we are mindful of, and our subconscious thoughts are the habitual ways of thinking that we are not aware of. Our intimate cognitive processes impact the energy levels within this field, as you have seen in the belief cycle. Our thoughts can be positive, having a high vibration, or they can be negative, having a lower vibration.

These vibrations directly impact a person's energy and, ultimately, their results. As individuals evolve their negative thoughts to those that are positive, they will generate more energy within their cognitive zone. I encourage you to go back and re-read the above section on inner dialogue to help with your assessment of the potential energy leaks in this zone. Any negative thought or emotion is an energy leak.

Physical Energy Zone

Two components make up your physical or body energy zone and include your physique's internal and external impacts. How you treat your body internally and externally will be reflected by the condition in which your physical body operates. Components impacting the internal physical energy levels include the items you put into your body, such as food, water, and toxins. The external impacts on the physical energy zone include exercise, sleep, and other self-care regimes. The nature of what you do to your body will create the nature of your results, whether it be enriching or draining. It is essential to take the time to study your body and learn what fuels your energy and what drains your energy tank. Let's look at how we can understand the energy leaks we may be experiencing in the physical energy zone through acknowledgment and assessment.

Acknowledge: The first step is to identify if you have an energy leak within your physical energy. The following indicators identify leaks: feeling tired, lacking ambition, slow, groggy, and physical pain. It is critical to be as honest and transparent with yourself to truly understand if there exists one of these feelings described above.

Assessment: The next step is to work on identifying the

triggers of these energy leaks. If you notice yourself feeling one or more of the slowed-down vibrational energies, you must determine the root causes. Some of the common culprits include but are not limited to:

- Having an unbalanced diet is consuming too much or too little of something. For example, complex carbs, such as wheat, grains, and corn, require more energy to break down. For some people, consuming too much of these food items will sabotage their energy levels. Consider journaling your regular food intake to understand potential energy leaks concerning diet. Take the time to investigate and study your body to learn what fuels you and what drains you.
- Additionally, you must assess the toxins you may be consuming, such as alcohol, nicotine, drugs, and even caffeine. These items have a significant impact on our energy levels, hormones, the chemicals in our brains, and the body's automatic functions.[1] Make a list of these toxic substances you are consuming to understand better how your physical energy levels are being impacted.
- Regular fitness regimes create a healthier physical body by reducing excess weight and increasing the strength of joints and muscles while improving bodily functions such as the circulatory system. You will experience increased blood flow, oxygen intake, and energizing hormone levels. Additionally, you will reduce the lower energy outcomes of disease, injury, and mental health concerns. Exercise is known to combat diabetes, anxiety, depression, arthritis, and many more physical and mental ailments. You can relieve your body of these energy leaks by managing and eliminating health concerns. To ensure you are getting enough of this energy-boosting component, I encourage

you to assess the amount and type of physical exercise you are partaking in.

- Ensuring you are getting enough rest or downtime is essential to recharge. You cannot expect to run at full speed without taking moments to fuel up. Numerous studies have shown that a lack of sleep can lead to many health issues, including obesity, diabetes, lowered immune system, cardiovascular disease, and many more ailments.[2] Sleep issues can arise due to active lifestyles, work schedules, family activities, and health disorders. We must take the time to get the rest we need despite our hectic lifestyles. Consider what these recharging moments are for you. They may include: sleep, yoga, reading a book, going for a walk, or listening to a podcast.

- Also, consider the self-care regimes you have implemented in your life. Do you partake in chiropractic care, massage therapy, acupuncture, or stretching? These personal care regimes leave the body feeling in alignment and recharged, contributing to the overall energy we experience.

Environmental Energy Zone

This energy zone goes beyond our physical bodies and encompasses our homes, workplaces, extracurricular activities, places of worship, and school. These environments have numerous components that can significantly impact our energy levels. At first, this energy zone may seem like you have limited control over the influences of each environment; however, this is a false limitation that many individuals place upon themselves. These limitations provide an excuse to avoid the work involved in protecting your energy levels. You cannot control the types of individuals or the outside stimuli in each environment. Still, you can learn to set boundaries and develop mental toughness to reduce the external influences on your mind. Additionally, you can limit your time in specific settings that you consider an energy leak in your life. Let's look at some considerations to make as you complete your self-assessment.

Acknowledge: Just like your cognitive and physical energy zones, you must first identify if you have an energy leak due to your environmental circumstances. Discovering if you have an energy leak outside of your body and mind is simply taking the time to complete self-evaluations of your energy levels as you are in different settings. Suppose you experience similar feelings to those of having a physical or mental energy leak. In that case, you must dig deeper into what is causing your stamina depletion in these settings.

Assessment: Subsequently to recognizing and identifying the environments in which you observe lower or drained energy levels, the next phase is to identify the root causes. A great assessment tool is to evaluate the presence of lower frequency emotions and feelings and evaluate what or whom is the trigger for these lower energy experiences. It is critical to emphasize the difference between identifying the root cause and blaming someone or something for your emotions and feelings. Identifying the root cause reveals the lower energy thoughts you have allowed to take hold of your life. I implore you to consider the following points to determine your environmental energy leaks.

- An individual's association has a significant effect on their energy levels. I encourage you to take note of your thoughts and feelings when around the various individuals in your association. Identify those that inspire you and those that drag you down. This evaluation will help you understand why you may feel drained in specific environments.

- Take time to assess the events and activities you are participating in. Some may be considered a significant energy leak, while others are soothing and fueling. Make a list of the activities you find yourself losing energy over and identify if it is because of the event itself or other factors such as people or input.
- There are many other possible toxic impacts from your environment, such as news, media, tv shows, podcasts, and books. These components can impact your inner dialogue and become a significant energy leak to your cognitive zone, as you have read earlier. Make a list of the environments with these other negative inputs through your assessment.

Self-Esteem & Egotism

Self-Esteem

Since self-esteem or admiration is rooted in how we view ourselves, including our perceptions of personal appearance and performance, it is crucial to understand the nature of our esteem. You can look at admiration as a sliding scale where the far left represents low self-esteem and the far right represents high self-esteem. In the middle is balanced self-esteem, where you have a healthy view of yourself. Taking a deeper look at esteem can aid in our understanding of the beliefs within our inner worlds. As individuals move towards a balanced view of themselves, they will promote an evolutionary environment for psychological change and growth.

Healthy Esteem

Having healthy esteem means that you see yourself as someone valuable and whole as you exist. You are compassionate towards yourself, accepting every characteristic that makes you who you are. Healthy esteem will enhance your sense of purpose, bringing more peace into your life. It is important to remember that our self-assessments, respect, worth, and opinions are due to the inner programming of our minds. When we alter our stored beliefs and thoughts regarding self, we can influence our self-worth and self-esteem. Healthy self-esteem is critical to fostering mental well-being, feeling that we are good, worthy, and respected. Those that achieve this balance of self contain a high degree of faith, confidence, and knowledge without going over the top with their need for recognition or approval. These Individuals are usually happy, selfless, caring, upbeat, and self-reliant. As individuals work on improving their views of self, they will begin to foster an environment conducive to transforming other stored beliefs.

Unhealthy Esteem

Unhealthy self-esteem is expressed by two extremes: high self-esteem and low self-esteem. Individuals with an unhealthy view of themselves have allowed an imbalance into their lives, either seeing themselves as above others or not seeing themselves as enough. Those who have high esteem are over the top, confident in their abilities, conceited, arrogant, and self-centered. These individuals are dominated by ego, believing they are always right and tend to be very defensive when others think they may be wrong. Low self-esteem is present when an individual is filled with doubt and concern for one's ability to succeed, feeling inadequate and worthless. Individuals with a poor view of themselves are typically sad, deflated, critical, and lack confidence. Studies have shown that low self-esteem precludes mental health concerns such as anxiety and depression.[3] Much like those with high self-esteem, those with low self-esteem have numerous coping mechanisms that show up in the form of ego. Let's look at the different unhealthy expressions of ego and how it plays a role in limiting our beliefs.

Egotism

The ego plays an integral role in an individual's perceptions, knowledge, identifications, and personality. As defined, ego is your conscious mind, the part of your identity that you consider yourself.[4] A healthy level of egotism is beneficial to handle the daily stresses of life. When individuals have an inflated ego or thoughts of self-importance, they usually operate out of comparison, judgment, and self-interest. Problems arise when one allows unhealthy levels of ego into their life, misidentifying one's self as their body, accomplishments, possessions, reputations, and thoughts of being separate.[5] For simplicity, when I refer to ego throughout this book, the context I am referring to is an unhealthy level of egotism.

Ego needs validation, approval, and accolades to continue its domination quest. Thoughts of egotism thrive off of control and mastery of others. Any time you value something over peace, your ego is in control. As you have read earlier, low or high esteem is the ultimate breeding ground for ego. Understanding the toxicity of these thoughts of self-importance can be better understood by reviewing the different ingredients of these self-centered thoughts. Gleaning from many educational resources, including Wayne Dyer's book, *The Power of Intention*, and Eckart Tolle's book *A New Earth*, I have summarized what I see as the six main characteristics of ego and the thoughts of identification that accompany each of these traits.

Accumulation and Ownership of Things

Individuals with this form of ego present in their life misidentify who they are as their material possessions. If you struggle with thoughts like "I am what I have," you have allowed your material items to determine your value. If this is the dominating thought you experience, what happens if you lose everything? Does that mean you are nothing? Our ego wants us to believe that all the money and worldly things we accumulate are what make us whole. Our higher selves know that we are not our possessions. In Wayne's words, we come into this world with nothing and will leave this world with nothing. To move towards your higher self, you must go through the following steps:

Acknowledge: The first step towards growth and evolution is identifying the presence of ego or self-importance rooted in the attainment of material items. Do you have any of the following thoughts: I am what I acquire, and what I have is mine. My money, possessions, and accumulations define my worth. If I have little, I am less than those who have more. If the items I own are more expensive, I am superior to those who own cheaper things. The value of my possessions determines my worth as a person.

Assessment: Next, you must take an in-depth inventory of what possessions you wrap your identity around.

- If you sense yourself experiencing a high when attaining an object followed by anxiety or fear of losing it, you have allowed this type of ego to enter your life.
- Upon discovering the material items you find yourself attached to, consider the reason for your attachments. This evaluation will require reviewing your past and present. Make notes of when you noticed this face of ego controlling your life. Were there events or circumstances

leading up to this point that may be considered a root cause?

Achievements and Weaknesses

Individuals whose self-worth is tied to their success or failures have allowed this form of egotism to penetrate their minds. If you have the dominating thoughts of "I am what I achieve" or "I am my weaknesses," then I'll ask a familiar question, what happens when you lose the ability to continue to achieve? Does that once again mean you are nothing? We are most connected to our higher spiritual self the moment we enter this world, and we do not come into this world "doing" anything.

Acknowledge: Identify if you have the presence of thoughts where you believe your achievements or lack of accomplishments determine who you are as a person, ultimately impacting your self-worth and esteem. Assess if you have any of the following beliefs: I am what I have accomplished or failed at. My successes and failures are dictators of my self-worth. If I fail at something, I am bad. If I succeed, I am good. My career and extracurricular activities are who I am. Without them, I am nothing. My weaknesses must be hidden from society at all costs, for they will establish my value as less than those who do not have deficiencies.

Assessment: Here, you must dig past the existence of these ego-filled thoughts and feelings to understand which accomplishments you have tied your self-worth and identity to.

- To help with this evaluation, make a list of your accomplishments and how you would feel if they were taken away. It is normal to recognize thoughts of sadness, frustration, or even anger. What is concerning is if you think you are less of a person without these successes.

- Knowing the achievements you have wrapped your identity around will help you dig into your past and present to reveal the roots of these thoughts. Developing this awareness will require intimacy and vulnerability with yourself. Evaluate what events or circumstances led up to your attachment to success?

Personality & Reputation

Thoughts of our past defining who we are, with concerns of "I am my personality and what others think of me," is giving power to the egotistical self. Labeling ourselves based on our genetic makeup, temperament, and character traits prevents us from stepping outside the box we have put ourselves into. If we keep looking in the rearview mirror while driving to see if someone is watching, eventually, we will lose control and crash. Let's take a look at some things to consider as we take an inventory of this face of egotism.

Acknowledge: Here, we must take the time to evaluate whether or not you find yourself worried about your characteristics, your past and present, or concerned about what others think of you. Do you find yourself overwhelmed by the need to please others? Recognize if any of the following psychological complexes exist as a part of your beliefs and thoughts: I am my personality and what others think of me. My actions and attitudes make up my reputation, which others judge. I was born with fixed personality traits, and they define me. My past determines how others will see me. The need to please people drives my decision-making more than how I feel internally.

Assessment: Once you have exposed the exact thoughts and attachments over your personality and reputation, you can move forward with your self-assessment of these egoic thoughts.

- Reflect on your past and present. Seek to discern the moments your misidentification of who you are as a person is dependent on your personality and reputation began. Can you remember a time free from this face of ego?
- Do you recall specific individuals in your life that struggle with this form of egotism? Is it possible these individuals were a primary influence in the way you view your personality and reputation? Consider the experiences or outcomes that contributed to creating this egotism in yourself. From here, you will be able to identify the areas of your life that may require growth and elevation.

Physical Attributes

Our lower energy selves are attuned to the physical dichotomies that dominate our society, focusing on comparisons and judgments, spurring thoughts of "I am separate from everyone." Our egos feed off thoughts of competition with labels such as winners vs. losers, big vs. small, tall vs. short, fast vs. slow, beautiful vs. ugly, strong vs. weak, and wrong vs. right. When we engage in these contradictions and labels, we feed the ego's need for separation from others and our environments. As you look to understand this face of ego, here are some things to contemplate.

Acknowledge: Evaluate if you are experiencing the need to compare, judge, criticize and label others. Do you notice the presence of these lower energy thoughts: My body makes up who I am. My body defines me. My physical appearance determines the amount of success I will experience in all areas of my life. Some people are beautiful and strong, while others are ugly and weak. I am more or less of a person because of my physical attributes. If you recognize these thoughts intertwined within your mental complexes, I encourage you to move on to the next assessment step.

Assessment: As you recognize the existence of egotism fueled by your misidentifications tied to your body, consider the below suggestions to complete your intimate evaluations.

- Make a list of the dichotomies present in your thought processes. Begin to ask yourself when did you first notice their presence? How was your upbringing, and was this form of ego present then? Can you remember a time when you were free from this ego?
- Contemplate the environments of your work, home, and extracurricular activities. Do you notice the presence of comparison, judgments, blaming, or criticizing?
- Take inventory of your past and present environments that may have contributed to your toxic thoughts of the physical. Make a list of them.

Separation

When you believe in your separateness from your desires and outcomes, you are also saying that you have no control over the results that you create. If this is the case, you have fallen into a belief cycle controlled by outside influences, circumstances, and others. Recalling the belief cycle, the outcomes in your life result from your beliefs and thoughts. This psychological process confirms that we are connected to the manifestations we experience.

Acknowledge: Here, you must complete a self-evaluation of your internal beliefs around your capabilities to create what you desire in your life. Do you believe you are separate from all that is missing? Do you consider particular desires out of your hands or impossible to attain? Those plagued by this egotism have thoughts: I am disconnected from people and what's missing in my life. I must dominate and control my environment and others to achieve success rather than work unitedly. If I do not dominate others, then others will overpower me. I am more or less important than those around me. Division of humanity is normal, and some people are better than others. Some are right, while others are wrong. If any of these thoughts lie within your mind, you may have allowed this self-centered ego to blur your authentic essence and capabilities.

Assessment: Identifying beliefs of separation from the outcomes of your life is the first step towards elevating your thoughts while eliminating the hold this type of ego has on your life. As you complete your review, consider some of the following suggestions to help with this process.

- Identify the specific desires, tasks, or outcomes that you see as disconnected from yourself that you believe are impossible to attain.
- Why do you see these noted aspirations as separate from you? As you think back to your early programming years, do you notice environments that fostered division? How about your present life? Do you recognize this egotism present in environments and other individuals around you?
- This process can be overwhelming for some as these ingrained thoughts can be rooted in past wounds. These hurts may have led to a poor self-image, a lack of belief, and low self-esteem, all of which can lead to a life full of disconnection.

Independence from a Creator or God

When I talk about God throughout this book, I refer to the one and all divine creator responsible for the energy flowing through all of us. I am not speaking to a religious or specific God but rather an all-encompassing creator since there can only be one. Going back to an individual's relationship with God, when they have thoughts of disunity from our creator, they have fostered an environment that breeds ego. Ego and God cannot co-exist; therefore, separation becomes the ego's primary objective. When there is an existence of egoic thoughts, you have allowed your lower self to dominate your higher spiritual self. In this state, we have lost the intimate and authentic perception of ourselves, viewing who we are as all the different faces of ego. Here are some key points to evaluate as you assess this expression of ego.

Acknowledge: The intimate process of assessing one's own spiritual beliefs can be daunting for some. It is an essential step in understanding your thoughts around your connectedness and oneness with the source of our being. If you unwrap any thoughts of separation or disconnect from God during your discovery process, then I encourage you to move on to assessing these thoughts in further detail. Common beliefs for those who have allowed this form of ego to take over include: Since I am separate from God, my worthiness depends on pleasing God and meeting the higher powers' expectations. I will get special treatment if I act according to God's rules. I can handle this life journey independently; I do not need God.

Assessment: Taking the time to understand our authentic and deeply rooted beliefs is imperative to understanding and growing our connection with God. Here you must be as honest as you can, knowing that we all are on a unique spiritual journey.

- Take the time to evaluate and acknowledge whether your beliefs are true to you or if others have planted them. Do not be afraid to experience other faiths to see what resonates with your soul.
- Reflect on both your past and present. Have you experienced these toxic thoughts of division through your environments or others? Have you closed yourself off from sharing God's wisdom?
- Understand that there is a difference between having faith and truly knowing God. Only through experiences can you develop this knowledge of a higher power or creative force that resides in all of us. Are you open to receiving this divine guidance in your life? If not, why?

Summary of Egotism

If you recognize the existence of one or more of the six different unhealthy expressions of ego present in your life, and if you desire to eradicate these thoughts, you must take an accurate and in-depth inventory of the egotism that is dominating your mind. I would encourage writing these six points out on paper and reviewing them each day by asking yourself, "what thoughts and actions rooted in ego were present today?" This self-assessment will be an ongoing review as different situations can trigger or pull out other egotistical thoughts. I would also encourage you to consider seeking the perspective of someone you trust to share a truthful evaluation of the presence of ego. It is crucial to remember an outside perspective can reveal potential blind spots that you may have in your life.

Ignorance & Knowledge

At this point, you have learned that an individual's stored beliefs are made up of their own knowledge and experiences or through the opinions of others. Knowing this, we can then infer that if our knowledge changes, so too will our beliefs. Understanding and accepting this conclusion means that we must acknowledge our own ignorance. We do not know everything, and we begin to recognize the importance of knowledge gathering to bring clarity to the unfamiliar by accepting this.

A great example of this is the scenario we covered earlier where two individuals face the decision to snorkel at the Great Barrier Reef. If the individual who fears sharks becomes open to receiving new information and begins to educate themselves, they will very likely alter their stored beliefs. Their new thought complex will involve understanding the risks and behaviors associated with sharks. These altered beliefs will now encompass the latest thoughts and emotions created through the data gathering stage.

Acknowledge: As you encounter situations, events, or outcomes in your life, take the time to review your own rooted beliefs. I encourage you to ask yourself if you know all the facts regarding the beliefs you have formed. Have you gone down the path of discovery with each of these beliefs?

Assessment: As you become more open and aware of your ignorance, you will begin to lift the limitations you have placed upon your knowledge. You can now start to discover who you are and what beliefs you hold. Here are some thought-provoking questions to ask as you look towards understanding where you are at with the value you place around knowledge.

- What beliefs do you hold firmly regardless of new information provided and why?
- Considering your upbringing, was there a value placed around being open to new ideas and information?
- Do you embrace new beliefs as new data is presented?
- Are you willing to accept the possibility that your current belief system may be built off of an incomplete set of data?
- Do you have access to reputable data and sources to help expand your knowledge? News, media, and opinion-based articles are not reputable sources, and it would be best to rely solely on the experts in the field you are gathering data from.

Summary

During your self-assessment and taking inventory of where you are at, it is imperative to understand your beliefs and thoughts and understand why you have the psychological processes that you do. In addition to the early programming we all encounter, you will have other components contributing to your current belief system. Perhaps your beliefs are influenced by habitual negative self-talk, or you may be full of energy leaks, partaking in energy-draining activities with lower frequency stimulants. Additionally, you may recognize that you have an unhealthy level of self-esteem containing dominating thoughts of egotism. Or, you have acknowledged the presence of ignorance and a lack of information contributing to some of your beliefs. Whichever you identify as contributors to your negative views and thoughts, they can be altered and elevated to those of a higher frequency. As you keep reading, I will guide you through a process of deepening this evaluation and educating you on how you can alter your beliefs and thinking habits, which ultimately will lead to achieving the results you desire in your life.

The pertinent questions now become: can you let go of your need to control the narratives present in other individuals' minds? Can you stay in your lane, focusing on elevating your own beliefs, thoughts, emotions, responses, and outcomes? Are you willing to take ownership and let go of the self-centered egotism that has crept up in your life? The answers to these questions of personal focus and self-growth are critical as they determine the outcomes. It has become prominent throughout our nations for the media, government, and citizens to attempt to control each individual's thoughts and narratives, as seen throughout the pandemic. There is a pandemic of the collective ego taking over control, where comparison, judgment, and criticizing each other have become the norm. Just because someone thinks differently does not make them right or wrong, better or worse. It just makes them human.

Now that we have taken the time to walk through an inventory assessment of our past and present let's invest some time in summarizing everything we have learned through our discovery process, using our hierarchy of needs. In the next chapter, we will use the COVID-19 pandemic in our summary process to show how this review is completed. Remember that this type of assessment can be completed at any point in your life, not just through a difficult time and not just through the trying times of the pandemic. I use it as an example to personify the abstract ideas I've presented and humanize them so they are easy to implement in your everyday life.

> "Life is divided into three terms - that which was, which is, and which will be. Let us learn from the past to profit by the present, and from the present, to live better in the future." ~ William Wordsworth

CHAPTER 6

Taking Inventory: Assessing the Hierarchy of Needs

The last few chapters have focused on the second step of activating change in your life, *Taking an Inventory*. As you have learned, this process requires an intimate and authentic review of your past and present to understand where you are today and how you got there. Due to the significant amount of discovery required at this phase, it is advantageous to summarize these findings in a way that helps you understand and prioritize the areas of your life that require growth. To help you with this process, I will use Maslow's Hierarchy of needs to aid in summarizing the impacts of the Coronavirus pandemic. I use the pandemic as an example to show you how to apply the hierarchy of needs in your life. Again, this tool can be applied to everyone's lives at all times, not just during the pandemic. Additionally, this is not the only resource you can use. I also encourage you to harness your own values system or critical pillars of your life to help you in your assessment.

COVID-19 Impact on Our Hierarchy of Needs

As events unfolded, including the actions and responses by the media, government, big health organizations, and healthcare professionals, our hierarchy of needs was left in shambles. Our basic needs, psychological needs, and self-fulfilling needs became threatened at many different stages during the pandemic and continue to be as we are still currently walking through this time. Even as this horrendous event becomes one of the past, it will haunt many individuals for years to come if they allow it. Remember, we get to choose which events and circumstances we hold onto. As you continue to read about the devastation from COVID-19 or any other tumultuous event, keep in mind that you can overcome any of these hindrances as you consciously apply the teachings throughout this book.

Basic Needs: Physiological & Safety Needs

Physiological Needs

Our physical needs are essential to survival at the fundamental level, and these needs include air, food, water, clothing, shelter, sex, and rest. As you have learned in the preceding chapters, these needs were impacted and jeopardized for many individuals.

Food

Initially, significant fears of the virus led to individuals hoarding and stocking up on consumable items, including food, drinks, health and hygiene products, and many more. Shelves in grocery stores were empty, creating a snowball effect of inducing more fear. For some, their basic needs of food and water were threatened.

Shelter

Many individuals experienced an immense financial strain as jobs were lost and businesses closed. Although the government stepped in to help provide monetary aid, this took time. For some, this help came too late. As many individuals used up their savings accounts, the lack of financial power inevitably led to homes foreclosing, impacting their need for shelter.

Rest

The stress and anxieties that infiltrated our homes resulted in many individuals' lack of rest and sleep. With the numerous uncertainties that plagued our minds, our bodies were in a constant state of flight or fight mode, robbing individuals of their need for rest.

Physical Health

Closures of fitness facilities put the health of our physical bodies at risk as gyms, sports, and other physical activities were suspended. Individuals could no longer continue with their health regimes, causing disruptions to their body's health.

Safety Needs

Our feelings of being safe and secure consist of two contributors to our overall safety needs and include our physical and economic security. The concerns about our safety through COVID-19 are broken up into these two categories below:

Physical Safety

Impacts on our physical safety include war, disasters, violence, and illness. The pandemic consisted of numerous safety concerns, contributing to the hindrance of an individual's overall safety.

Coronavirus Threat

Initially, the media and governments portrayed COVID-19 as a virus that could wipe out the world. The impact of this assumption brought with it grave consequences. Individuals developed debilitating fears, leading to severe anxiety and depression.

Rumors of Biological War

Rumors and concerns about the virus being a biological weapon caused even more havoc in our communities. Thoughts of "is our world going to war?" festered in many individuals' minds.

Vaccine Threat

The rapid vaccine development and rollout created anxiety around the safety of these new inoculations. Additional concerns involved a lack of transparency regarding the mechanisms used in delivering the vaccine throughout the body. Vaccine waning after six months, along with the inability to prevent infection and spread, had many individuals wondering, why is there such a big push for a vaccine with limited effectiveness? Furthermore, as adverse side effects from the vaccines started to surface, more individuals developed skepticism around the safety profile of these new inoculations.

Mandates Threat & Government Pressures

Various government leaders across the globe fueled the division within their communities through their bold statements, pressures, and actions regarding an individual's choice to get vaccinated or not. Countries rolled out different degrees of mandates, squeezing those who chose not to be vaccinated. Those who feared the vaccine developed anxieties and experienced threats to their physical health and freedom of choice.

Economic Safety

An individual's economic safety is very different from their physical safety. Here an individual's security is reliant on establishing financial and personal protection.

Job Security

As the government activated restrictions, it became mandatory for businesses to close their doors, resulting in people losing their jobs. Numerous companies could not handle the extended period of lockdowns and went bankrupt, leaving the owners in a state of a financial crisis.

Financial Security

Some people burned through their savings quickly without a steady income stream, resulting in financial distress. They lost their current stream of income and they lost their life savings.

Personal Security

Initially, the closure of businesses, mask mandates, and social gathering restrictions infringed on our typical day-to-day life. These constraints manifested concerns about losing our freedom of choice and living our lives freely. As the events unfolded across the globe, censorship of professionals, varying degrees of vaccine mandates, and some countries requiring vaccine passports led to even more concern for losing individual freedoms.

Psychological Needs: Social & Esteem Needs

Social Needs

Our psychological needs began to suffer because the world became laser-focused on meeting the basic and lowest level of needs. Individuals became more focused on surviving vs. thriving during this pandemic, significantly impacting their social needs. An individual's need for love, respect, and belonging is foundational to the overall fulfillment of their social necessities.

The following events contributed to the starvation of connection, which ultimately contributed to our globe's poor mental health condition.

Closure of Extracurricular Activities

Our need for connection was first impacted by the closure of businesses that provided extracurricular activities, social meeting locations, churches, schools, and support groups. Subsequently, these activities fell into a conditional open status, which depended on vaccination and infection rate. Continuous opening and closing of social gathering activities repressed moments of connection individuals would feel.

Isolation & Stay at Home Orders

Social gathering restrictions and stay-at-home orders isolated individuals from family and friends for extended periods, further adding to the disconnection felt in our society. Social judgment plagued our communities, further impacting our choices to see family and friends.

Lengthy Quarantine Periods

The lengthy quarantine periods significantly impacted social needs, leading to poor mental health conditions. The anxieties and depression experienced were exasperated by the closure of psychological support groups combined with isolation mandates from personal support groups.

Separation & Division

The opposing narratives painted by the government and media, pinning vaccinated individuals against the unvaccinated, created even more division in our communities, negatively impacting one's sense of belonging. It became a war between friends and family based on vaccination status, which contributed to our discontent feelings across our nation.

Esteem Needs

An individual has a combination of lower esteem and higher esteem needs, which are essential to ensuring a healthy and balanced level of esteem. The lower esteem comprises external validations, acknowledgment, and respect from others. Higher esteem includes how we view ourselves and our self-belief, self-respect, self-worth, self-confidence, and independence. Many individuals found their esteem slipping to an unhealthy level as their inner dialogue, energy levels, egotism, and openness to understanding diminished.

Inner Dialogue

An individual's self-speech has the power to pull someone above any unfavorable external circumstances, or it can drag them down along with it. Evidently, many individuals allowed their minds to slip into negative thought processes. Statistics inarguably show the extensive increase in psychological health concerns, anxiety, and depression.

Stimulus & Energy Levels

All of our energy zones, the cognitive, physical, and environmental, had slipped into lower frequencies, creating a fertile environment for psychological health issues, including low self-worth & esteem.

Cognitive Energy Zones experienced a drop in energy levels while our inner dialogue and emotions were bred out of negativity, creating energy leaks within our mental zone.

Physical Energy Zones became depleted as the loss of our physical health regimes spurred laziness and inactivity leading to weight gain. Stress contributed to unhealthy eating habits exasperating physical illness concerns. Additionally, many individuals turned to substance use and even substance abuse to help cope with the circumstances they found themselves in. This consumption negatively impacted our overall health, draining the energy from our lives.

Environmental Energy Zones became infested with toxic stimulants that added fuel to our negative thoughts. Judgmental associations, including the media, government, coworkers, friends, and family, fostered the collective ego to take root. Our environmental influences grabbed onto any fear-inducing and criticizing news stories, articles, social media, and ads. Our surrounding energy levels were pulled into lower frequency vibrations, creating a significant energy leak.

Self-Esteem & Egotism

With unhealthy levels of egotism being the consequence of poor esteem, one can conclude that it was only a matter of time before this form of ego began to flourish and spread like wildfire. It appears out of nowhere, spreading rapidly, destroying all beauty that existed before its presence. This unstoppable force is what happened with the self-importance that has thrived during the pandemic. Ego and fears infested the minds and thoughts of many, encouraging individuals to misidentify their self-worth as their accumulations, achievements, personalities, reputations, physical appearance, and views of separation and independence from God. Those who allow ego to control their lives allow division, disrespect, comparison, judgments, and criticisms to manifest, naturally diminishing their self-portrait.

Ignorance & Knowledge

Due to the initial shock and paralyzing impact of the Coronavirus outbreak, individuals leaned heavily on others to provide updates and information. These sources of information included media, governments, large healthcare organizations, and healthcare professionals. Issues arose when the media took advantage of our nation's emotions, playing off the existing fear and turning the information gathering process into a high-stress activity. To add to this, the apparent divide between our political leaders and healthcare professionals created more confusion, leaving individuals feeling lost. Who would they turn to now in search of factual and evidence-based information? To make matters worse, many individuals became so fixed within their mindsets that they were not open to the discovery process, leaving them in a state of ignorance.

Self-Fulfillment Needs

Self-Actualization Needs

The suffering of our psychological needs was a by-product of our nation's shift from an abundance mindset to a scarcity mentality. One cannot transition to self-actualization until our social and esteem needs are met, moving us into a prosperous psyche. Individuals who reach this stage have accomplished living their life free from a self-centered ego and prejudice, focusing on creating abundance and higher awareness. The implications and overall collapse of this level of growth during the pandemic resulted from our lower needs being unfulfilled.

Presence of Ego

The presence of ego in many of our homes hindered our abilities to achieve self-fulfillment. When our minds become embroiled with lower energy thoughts, the results are negative, pulling us further from reaching our true potential.

Lack in Purpose

The dramatic shifts shook the direction or purpose of our lives, altering the areas in which we focus our growth. When lower-level needs are distressed, and we allow our thought processes to sink to lower frequencies, we suffocate the purpose and burning desires we have to reach for self-fulfillment.

Scarcity Focus

Focusing on survival reduced our abilities to transcend successful outcomes. Once again, what you focus your attention on, is what expands, and you cannot create growth out of insufficiencies.

Summary

Understanding the collective impact of each hindrance within the five levels of needs can bring about a holistic understanding of how each individual got to where they are at. Clearly, there exists a deep connection between the stages of growth where an individual's needs overlap in one's journey to higher awareness. To help actualize this journey, I've used the pandemic as an example. To visually see the impacts of the Coronavirus on our hierarchy of needs, I have summarized the impacts in Figure 4.

Figure 4: COVID-19 Impacts on our
Personal Hierarchy of Needs

Now that you have experienced what it looks like to complete a detailed review of the past and present using the Coronavirus as an example, you can now complete your own assessments, creating an inventory of your past and present. I suggest using a journal and going through each section yourself. It is paramount to approach this in-depth review without personal judgment, criticisms, and regret in our assessments. We will use compassion and understanding towards ourselves to produce an open and authentic approach to our reviews. It is essential to understand that there is no such thing as a failure, but rather moments and opportunities for learning. Accepting this truth will create the security needed to evolve and change. As you complete Step 2 with activating lasting change, you are now ready to move on to Step 3, *Taking Ownership* of where you are at. Stepping into full accountability will require you to accept that you are the sole reason for your outcomes. There will be a mindset shift through this journey of taking responsibility. I will help you eliminate all thoughts of excuses and blaming, making up a fixed view on every aspect of life. As you discard these negative thoughts, I'll walk you through how you can replace them with those of accountability and ownership, ensuring a growth mindset prevails.

"Everything you do is based on the choices you make. It's not your parents, your past relationships, your job, the economy, the weather, an argument or your age that is to blame. You and only you are responsible for every decision and choice you make. Period." ~ Wayne Dyer

CHAPTER 7

Taking Ownership of Your Life:
The Two Different Mindsets

As you embrace your life experiences, you may endure moments of intense desires, with an internal knowing that your current circumstance is not where you long to be. These feelings are your intuition speaking to you, now is the time to invoke change within your life. Through the self-assessments and in-depth reviews of your past and present, it is normal to experience an overwhelmed feeling. At this point, many individuals find themselves paralyzed with inactivity; they are unsure where to begin this transformation journey. When you notice this paralysis, recognize that it is speaking to you: "slow down and take the necessary moments to accept responsibility for your past and present fully; only then can you begin to let those parts of you go. As you free up mental space, you will begin to manifest new thoughts and, resultantly, new outcomes" This means that you must acknowledge and embrace that your outcomes are made up of your beliefs and thoughts. You must fully accept that you are the gateway to these thoughts and that the emotions, level of energies (vibrations), actions, and outcomes you have experienced result from your thinking. You will eliminate all blame and take 100% ownership of your past, present, and now your future. The key here is that you cannot blame others, circumstances, or events for your past and present outcomes and expect that you can own your future. How you choose to exist in one area of your life is how you will be in all areas. You own every part of your life or give it away to others. I urge you to choose not to give it away to others and take your thoughts and actions into your own hands.

Once you have accepted accountability for the entirety of your life, you must begin letting go of your past to make room for your present and future. As hard as this may be for some, with their past wounds running deep, it would help if you found the forgiveness necessary to begin the process of healing. This forgiveness can be releasing others from the pain they have caused you or forgiving yourself for the suffering you have brought into your life. Absolution of all wrongdoings will free you from the past. This choice is crucial because if you are always looking in the rear-view mirror, you will not experience the present moments before you. Transformation and elevation in your life will only occur once you have been able to be truly present in every moment of your life.

The Two Mindsets and Their Impacts on Taking Ownership

Through this journey of *Taking Ownership,* there are mental components that foster an environment of accountability while others suppress it. The early programming years that we all experience through childhood influence our cognitive processes.

If we do not challenge or question these embedded thoughts, they can remain with us for a lifetime. Significant influences include an individual's associations, environment, culture, traditions, genetics, DNA, talents, and personality. All of these components can be positive experiences full of teachings, or they can be limiting factors that box in our minds and are ultimately a negative influence on us throughout life. These early childhood components can elevate or hold us back because they will shape our "natural" mental processes over time. When we are young, these circumstances influence how we think and act later in life. This disposition leads to two different mindsets: a fixed mindset or a growth mindset. Up to this point, in your inventory assessments, you have made a note of the varying thoughts and emotions present. What has not been considered is the condition of your mind when taking in these thoughts and feelings.

This chapter will dive into your mind's natural tendencies that have developed since birth and provide certain shades and colors to your thoughts. For example, consider comparing an optimistic individual to a pessimistic individual. Those with optimism ingrained in their mental complexes will see the world through a positive frame of mind, whereas the cynical individual will see the world through a negative frame of mind. These individuals can walk through the same experience and take away different thoughts and feelings. The optimistic individual will look for the good, whereas the pessimistic individual will search for the bad. Both individuals will see their experience as "truth." Each thought that we have is filtered through the experiences and influences we've had in our lifetime. This process speaks to the power that our thoughts have in affecting our experiences. Knowing that we all have a natural sway on our thoughts is crucial to evaluating your tendencies on this journey. Understanding our intrinsic psychological processes and identifying the natural pull of our minds is imperative in accepting full responsibility and taking ownership of the entirety of our existence. With this in mind, let's plunge into understanding the two different mindsets to see where you currently reside. You may notice a combination of the two dispositions, or you may notice that you sway one way more than the other. Whichever direction your conclusions lead to, remember that this chapter is all about *Taking Ownership*, and part of that is being true to yourself in your evaluations.

Fixed Mindset

Early Programming Years

Do you recall moments from your early childhood years when your parents or teachers encouraged or praised particular talents or traits you have? Or maybe you received an abundance of accolades for the successes you experienced and criticism for your failures? Or perhaps you were raised in a competitive environment where success should require little effort? If you have to try hard to succeed at something, that is considered a failure. Do you recall feeling judged based on your talents and that your worth depends on your flawless abilities? If you answered yes to any of these questions, then you most likely have experienced the workings of fixed-minded individuals in your life. A fixed mindset is rigid to change and believes that traits and talents are set in stone and cannot be altered or grown. The following assessment is this: have you allowed these fixed and rigid thoughts of others to determine your own natural pull, making up the character of your mind? In other words, have you become a fixed-minded individual yourself? In completing this review, let's take the time to understand the character traits of those with a fixed mindset.

Characteristics of a Fixed Mindset

As you have learned, a rigid mindset consists of thoughts and beliefs that you are either successful or unsuccessful based on your inherent traits that cannot be altered. The entirety of this mindset consists of many more characteristics, including:

- Talent is made up of effortless success, and ability should naturally show up.
- If you have to put the effort in or try at something, you have failed.
- Having the belief that an individual's capabilities are fixed; therefore, they must always "show up" and prove their abilities to the world.
- Fixed-minded individuals pursue easy tasks out of the fear of looking bad if they fail at something more challenging.
- They feel accomplished when they achieve perfection in their endeavors.
- Their feelings of worthiness rely on their abilities to be better than others, leading to ego dominating their lives as they live every experience as a competition.
- A fixed-minded individual facing failure will experience stress, depression, anxiety, and other mental health concerns. Their internal thought process is, "I have failed, so I am a failure."
- These individuals who have a fixed mindset and experience stress and anxiety may have developed an addiction to their circumstances. Recall that stress induces the "flight or fight" response causing addicting emotions and leading to a dependency on unhealthy environments, relationships, and circumstances.
- Negative and lower energy thoughts control these individuals' minds to handle failure by blaming others and making excuses.

- Some will go as far as cheating their way through life to avoid disappointment at all costs
- A fixed-minded individual dislikes the journey towards accomplishment because of the fear of failure and perfectionistic obsessions.

These traits of someone with a fixed mindset are some of the common ones I have seen in my research and personal experiences. Through your time of discovery, it is vital to identify the presence of any of these thoughts or characteristics that are intrinsically a part of your cognitive processes. Let's take things further and combine the fixed mindset characteristics listed above with the belief process discussed in Chapter 4. In Figure 5, you can see the thoughts, feelings, actions, and outcomes resulting from a rigid mentality. Take note of the undesirable behaviors and outcomes that transpire from this frame of mind: blame and unaccountability.

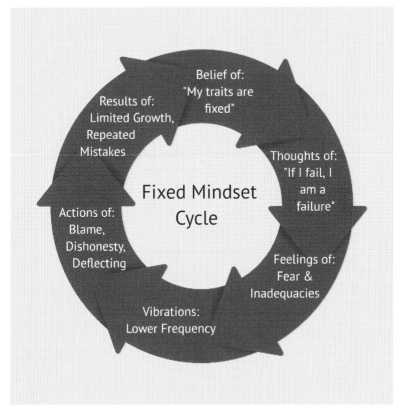

Figure 5: A Fixed Mindset: Individual's
Thought Process Towards Failure

If you notice a fixed mindset in all or some of your thought processes, I want you to know that this is normal. Most, if not all, individuals will have a mixture of both frames of mind. The key here is to identify the areas in which you have placed limitations upon yourself, creating this rigidity, and then work to exterminate these rigid ways of life, moving towards thoughts of growth. It is essential to understand that any fixed mindset has been established over time and places limitations on one's true potential, creating a false wall of "I cant's." It would be best to acknowledge that these thoughts may have been planted by someone else, but they have been nurtured and grown by yourself. Only you have the power to change them, and that, too, will take time to develop, but you must make a choice to begin.

An example to help you understand the falsehood of a rigid mindset and its unnatural way of thinking is the concept of developing skills. If we were truly born with fixed characteristics and abilities, then why do toddlers continue to work at learning to walk after they have failed numerous times? It would be rather silly if they stopped trying to walk after falling once, wouldn't it? So why do adults see challenges as bad, giving up when things get tough? We are all born with a desire to learn and grow, viewing challenges as something to overcome rather than avoid. As children get older and begin to communicate and understand words, the outside influences of our world put these limitations on us, and our own lack of self-awareness allows this fixed mindset to grow and dominate us. So, what if we were brought up in an environment free from constraints and full of thoughts of possibilities? Let's take a look at what this growth mindset entails.

Growth Mindset

Early Programming Years

Alternatively to the fixed mindset environment, a growth mindset is quite different. Instead of receiving praise based on your talents, do you recall experiencing appreciation based on your efforts? Or how about receiving encouragement rather than criticism during times of unfavorable outcomes? In experiencing failure, were your feelings and emotions disconnected from your self-worth? Did you believe that you were worthy regardless of your results? Were you raised in a cooperative environment where helping others was seen as a strength leading to success? If your answer is yes to one or more of the above questions, then you may have been exposed to the elements of a growth mindset environment. Limitations are absent within this growing mentality, where one can foster and develop skills and characteristic traits. Much like the fixed mindset, a growth mentality contains numerous characteristics that make up the evolutionary thoughts and beliefs that one may hold.

Characteristics of a Growth Mindset

As you have learned, individuals with a growth mindset believe that their character, abilities, and skills develop over time with effort and determination. Other beliefs held by growth-minded individuals include:

- You must put effort into any vocation you desire to succeed at.
- They believe that individuals' traits and skills are not fixed and can be changed if we wish to alter them.
- These individuals do not feel the need to prove themselves to others as they know their success will come if they stay dedicated to learning.
- Growth-minded individuals thrive during challenges and enjoy the problem-solving of complicated tasks.
- Feelings of achievement that they experience come with the positive results created through hard work and persistence.
- They believe their worth comes from who they are as a person rather than their accomplishments, successes, and failures. These individuals are free from unhealthy levels of egotism and have disconnected their worthiness from the results created in life.

- These individuals tend to have healthy self-worth and esteem, which reduces stress, anxiety, and depression concerns.
- Higher energy and positive thoughts drive these individuals to handle failure as a learning experience.
- These individuals have character traits of accountability and ownership over their lives.
- They accept responsibility for their losses without blame or excuses. They understand their outcomes are because of the choices they have made.
- They enjoy the journey of their pursuits, even if they experience failures along the way.

As you have read the components of a growth-minded individual, take note of those traits that are a part of your character. It is essential to continue to foster these developing traits, placing a priority on learning and development. Otherwise, you can easily slip into the frame of mind fixed with limitations placed upon your skills and abilities. Let's look at the thought process for individuals containing a growth mindset. Refer to Figure 6 to understand these individuals' thoughts, feelings, actions, and outcomes.

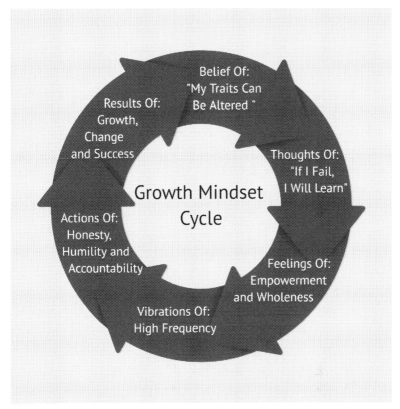

Figure 6: A Growth Mindset: Individual's
Thought Process Towards Failure

As one can see, there are many positive outcomes of having
an open and inviting mindset to change. Through your self-
assessments, if you notice the presence of this evolutionary
mindset, I encourage you to continue to foster and grow this
openness. Having a limitless mind and being genuinely open
to all possibilities will lead to the ultimate fulfillment you
desire. Remember, great desires require grand responsibility and
accountability.

Summary

Understanding the natural bend of our minds due to the early programming years and the differences between a fixed mindset and a growth mindset is crucial to growth and transformation. Through your assessments, you may identify a combination of fixed and growth mindsets, as most individuals do contain a mixture of the two. You may find yourself more open to growth in certain areas and closed off in others. You must understand that you can change the fixed mindset at any point in time through the process of autosuggestion you have learned. This transformation process will require a consistent and persistent effort as it will take time to rewire old ways of thinking and replace them with new and prosperous thoughts. *Taking Ownership* and responsibility for your life is the third step of activating change and owning your past, present, and future. Only then can you shift towards the fourth step in activating lasting change, *Creating a Plan and Take Action.* To grow from where you are to where you desire to be, you must make your intentions stand firm by backing them with a game plan. In the next chapter, we will review some thoughts and considerations to make as you develop your strategy for growth and success. This stage is integral to personal evolution as you are making a personal commitment to ensure ongoing development. We've done lots of work in preparation, now let's start making some plans today.

"Unless commitment is made, there are only promises and hopes; but no plans." ~ Peter F. Drucker

CHAPTER 8

Create a Plan and Take Action: Shift from Your Lower Self to Your Higher Self

In the pages leading up to this point, we have explored three fundamental components required for an individual to begin the process of elevation. These requirements are invisible to the outside world, involving an intimate process of internal assessments and transformations. If you recall, these three steps include:

- Step 1: Identifying your *Purpose Fueled by a Burning Desire* for change.
- Step 2: *Taking an Inventory* of your past and present.
- Step 3: Acknowledging and *Taking Ownership* of where you are at.

As an individual infuses openness, honesty, and depth with each of these foundational steps, they will establish a solid substructure, preparing them for Step 4, *Create a Plan and Take Action*. In this part of the process, you will begin to curate a plan that will result in a shift from your observed lower self to your desired higher self. The motivation to develop the plan is simple. Ask yourself: is where I am at with my life where I truly desire to be? In other words, does my burning desire match up with my inventory? If the answer is no, then it's time to work on creating a meaningful plan for change that you are willing to activate.

As you have learned earlier, you can use many different tools to help you identify the areas requiring growth, including but not limited to your own value system, purpose, vision, mission statements, and Maslow's Hierarchy of Needs. Using the data you have gathered, you can build your blueprint for propelling change in your life. To guide you with creating a plan, in this chapter, I will use a combination of our hierarchy of needs and an individual's values system sprinkled throughout to create a framework. You will be able to utilize the components within each level of growth that you have identified as holding you back to develop a personalized plan to transcend towards self-fulfillment. Knowing your current location and setting your GPS to your destination or burning desires will help you understand the path and changes required throughout each area of your life. You will notice that there may be overlap among each step for growth within your hierarchy and that the standard progression is not fixed. During each level of development, phase of planning, and actions to take, I have included three components to consider to develop a solid strategy for growth. I call these ingredients the three A's: *acknowledge, assessment and action.*

- *Acknowledgment* is purely the identification phase that you have walked through already, where you have recognized dissatisfaction is present in your life. This recognition is when you begin to fulfill Step 2, *Taking an Inventory.*

- *Assessment* is the evaluation of your current location compared to your desired destination. This analysis is where you continue to add to Step 2, *Taking an Inventory,* and fulfilling Step 3, *Taking Ownership.* You will complete this review through a series of questions that answer the 6 W's: What, When, How, Why, Where, and Who. This structure is a successful coaching technique that I have used to help clients dive deep into their personal assessments. I will refer to this as the 6W framework throughout the pages of this book.

- *Action* is the steps required to reach self-fulfillment. Here you will accomplish Step 4, *Creating a Plan and Taking Action.* You will also find Step 6, *Review and Assess,* will also be also be touched on. This process of taking action is supported by creating SMART goals: specific, measurable, attainable, relevant, and time-sensitive. This tool is a framework that I have also included as a part of my coaching methods. As individuals establish clarity on their goals and alterations required, they become propelled into action.

The structure of this plan was instrumental in transforming my life during the challenging times of the Coronavirus pandemic. You can implement it anytime as you move towards your best self. It is important to reiterate that the uniqueness of our journeys that led to where we are today will also lead to different choices, growth experiences, and paths. We all start from varying points in our journey to growth within our hierarchy of needs, which is OK. There is no such thing as competition for personal transformation, as there is an unlimited amount of change that we can all pursue. One's growth on their journey does not take away from the potential of another's. There are no final destinations; only pit stops along your adventure to personal realization. Even when you complete your action plans or reach specific goals for yourself, you will continue to reassess and make new plans.

Basic Needs: Physiological & Safety Needs

If you start your transformation journey here, at the basic needs, you will focus on satisfying your physical and safety necessities. These two levels of needs are intricately intertwined, and I will share more about their connectedness in a moment. It is critical to note the difference between experiencing fear and experiencing actual threats to these basic needs. For example, if we look at the basic need for food, ask yourself, are you worried about the lack of food, or are you experiencing the actual outcome of hunger and starvation due to having a lack of food? There is a significant difference between fearing and experiencing the actual result of that fear. As you note the concerns and fears present in your life, recognize that they are a cognitive component and will be discussed at the psychological level of your social and esteem needs. This section will address actual hindrances to the physical and safety necessities, not the fear of potentially occurring hindrances. It is also essential to recognize that there are numerous third-world countries where individuals experience many threats to their basic needs. In these cases, individuals may rely heavily on charitable organizations to help fulfill their physical and safety necessities. I encourage anyone in these situations to courageously accept the help from others when offered while elevating oneself to become self-reliant in meeting these basic needs. Now let's look at the physical and safety necessities that you must meet along your journey to self-fulfillment and what actions you can take to acquire them.

Physiological Needs

The physical needs are composed of air, food, water, clothing, shelter, and rest. These are the fundamental components of humanity's survival. As you embark on this growth journey, consider the necessary acknowledgments, assessments, and actions required.

Acknowledge: If you recognize a hindrance to your physical needs, you must decipher what requirements are lacking.

Assessment: During this review, you must complete a comparative study between your deficient needs and what complete fulfillment of these needs would look like. The gap identified between these two points will reveal the amount of work required to fulfill them. Here is a thought-provoking question sequence that involves answering the 6W's. Consider these questions in your evaluation process.

> **What** is contributing to a lack of fulfillment of your physiological needs?

> **When** did you first notice hindrances to these needs?

> **What** does the ultimate fulfillment of these needs look like for you?

> **How** can you begin to move towards fulfillment at this level of needs? In other words, what actions do you believe are necessary?

Why is it vital for you to elevate and fulfill these needs? (Reflect upon your purpose and burning desires to help answer this question)

Where might you experience obstacles or roadblocks to fulfilling these needs? (Use Chapter 9 on *Overcoming Obstacles* to help answer this question)

Who might you need support from to make these changes?

Action: Once you have identified the deprived physical needs and their causes and created a list of potential steps, you can begin developing your action plan. This plan will be supported by establishing SMART goals, and it will need to encompass your values, vision, and desires. Explore the following question sequence as you identify your actions steps:

Specific: What are your exact and particular goals for fulfilling your Physiological Needs?

Measurable: How will you track or measure your progress with these goals?

Attainable: Is each goal achievable for you, and do you have the power to activate them? Explain.

Relevant: Do these goals move you closer to reaching your greater vision? How?

Time Frame: When do you want to achieve each goal?

Safety Needs

As you evaluate your personal safety needs, there are two main components to ensure top security within this growth level: your physical and economic safety. It is vital to identify the actual risks versus the fears you are experiencing. All fears an individual experiences are their own thoughts and emotions at work, but it does not make it real just because you are experiencing it. A great example of this was the fears induced early in the pandemic. These anxieties were significant due to the assumption that COVID has a case fatality rate of 15.5%. Eventually, we learned the risks associated with the virus are significantly lower for young people who are not immunocompromised. As more data rolled out, the average fatality rate was around 2% before administering the vaccines.[1] Our original fear was insufficient due to limited data available. Once you can distinguish the concerns from the actual safety impacts, you can begin to grow in both your physical safety and economic safety needs.

Physical Safety

Your physical safety involves the security of your physical body from harm. It is relevant to mention that the level of protection someone experiences is very much influenced by the degree of poverty in their communities. Studies have shown a distinct connection between poverty and crime rates, indicating that living in a lower-income area can have more violence and physical threats to someone's safety.[2] This enhanced threat also applies to living in a third-world country or a country in conflict or war, where there is an apparent lack of physical security and basic safety needs. It is essential to emphasize that you can always change your degree of safety, no matter your current situation. If you genuinely desire growth towards your highest self, you must work to eliminate any limitations you may place upon yourself. Here are some suggested considerations to make as you look to improve your safety.

Acknowledge: First, you must identify if there is a real threat to your security, and this will require an openness to knowledge and discovery to aid in your conclusions. Take note of the specific safety threats you are experiencing.

Assessment: Next, we will complete an evaluation of the current state of your physical safety needs and your ideal condition. Through this review, I encourage you to reflect on the following points.

> **What** is contributing to a lack of fulfillment of your physical safety needs? These factors may include your personal engagements, surrounding environments, associations, and job.

> **When** did you first notice hindrances to these needs?

> **What** does ultimate fulfillment of your physical safety needs look like? Describe the environment in which you would be safe.

> **How** can you begin to move towards fulfillment at this level of needs? In other words, what actions do you believe are necessary?

> **Why** is it important for you to elevate and fulfill these needs? (Reflect upon your purpose and burning desires to help answer this question)

Where might you experience obstacles or roadblocks to fulfilling these needs? (Use Chapter 9 on *Overcoming Obstacles* to help answer this question)

Who might you need support from to make these changes?

Action: Through your analysis, you should have been able to identify your physical safety concerns, their root causes, and the changes you need to make. You are now ready to develop your plan of action to help create a safe environment for yourself. Contemplate the below questions to establish your SMART goals for elevating your physical safety needs.

Specific: What are your goals for fulfilling your physical safety needs?

Measurable: How will you track or measure your progress with these goals?

Attainable: Are these goals achievable for you, and do you have the power to activate them? Explain.

Relevant: Do these goals move you closer to reaching your greater vision? How?

Time Frame: When do you want to achieve each goal?

Economic Safety

Our overall security fulfillment relies not only on our physical safety but also on our economic safety, including security within your job, business, finances, and personal protection and preservation of our freedoms. This area of safety is also impacted by your environment, whether it's a first-world country or a third-world country. I will continue to emphasize the value of disposing of any constraints one may place upon themselves because of their environment, circumstances, and past. You are capable of achieving economic abundance and security if you are determined to make it happen. Now let's take a detailed look at these two different areas of economic safety and some considerations for growth.

Job, Business & Financial Security

Acknowledge: Having a secure income stream and financial security are significant contributors to an individual's sense of assurance and safety. If you have concerns regarding your job, business, or financial security through your assessments, it is crucial to identify if the risk is real. Again, we must decipher the difference between our fears and the actual experiences we are encountering.

Assessment: Once knowing the existence of an actual threat to either your job, business, or finances, the next step is to identify how you can increase or fulfill these security needs. Some thoughts to consider but are not limited to include:

What contributes to a lack of fulfillment of your job, business, and financial needs? Are these causes because of outside factors or your own habits and actions?

When did you first notice hindrances to these needs?

What does the ultimate fulfillment of these needs look like for you? What does your ideal economic safety look like for your job, business, and finances? Is there a specific job, business, or financial dollar value that would contribute to your overall security?

How can you begin to move towards fulfillment at this level of needs? In other words, what actions do you believe are necessary?

Why is it important for you to elevate and fulfill these needs? (Reflect upon your purpose and burning desires to help answer this question)

Where might you experience obstacles or roadblocks to fulfilling these needs? (Use Chapter 9 on *Overcoming Obstacles* to help answer this question)

Who might you need support from to make these changes?

Action: Knowing the limitations, root causes, and the ideal steps you must take to elevate your sense of security within your job, business, or finances, it's time to develop your blueprint for action. Here are some thoughts to consider throughout this development.

Specific: What are your goals for fulfilling your job, business, and financial needs?

Measurable: How will you track or measure your progress with these goals?

Attainable: Are these goals obtainable for you, and do you have the power to activate them? Explain.

Relevant: Do these goals move you closer to reaching your greater vision? How?

Time Frame: When do you want to achieve each goal?

Personal and Freedom Security

An individual's freedom and security involve living their life freely under the charter of rights, liberties, and the law. A major contributor to ensuring your overall safety needs are satisfied is experiencing feelings of safety and protection.

Acknowledge: Here, you must ask yourself, "Do I feel safe and secure to live my life free within the bounds of the laws, and are my rights protected under the law? Do I have any actual threats to my personal protection and rights as a human being?" A threat to one's personal and freedom security might include government overreach limiting your personal freedom of choice, closing a country's border, limiting free travel, and lethal force applied by law enforcement.

Assessment: If you have identified actual threats to your rights and freedoms, then we must assess the following:

What contributes to a lack of fulfillment of your personal protection and preservation of your freedom needs?

What does the ultimate fulfillment of these needs look like for you?

How can you begin to move towards fulfillment at this level of needs? In other words, what actions do you believe are necessary? Consider having a conversation with an independent professional operating under the law to understand this further.

Why is it important for you to elevate and fulfill these needs? (Reflect upon your purpose and burning desires to help answer this question)

Where might you experience obstacles or roadblocks to fulfilling these needs? (Use Chapter 9 on *Overcoming Obstacles* to help answer this question)

Who might you need support from to make these changes?

Action: Understanding your options to enhance your personal security may seem like a daunting task as you may feel you have limited control of this aspect of safety; this is not true, though. You have the power to enhance your security; it just may require bold decisions and actions to be taken. Here is the SMART goals question sequence to help you establish your empowering actions.

> **Specific:** What are your goals with fulfilling your personal protection and preservation of your freedom needs?

> **Measurable:** How will you track or measure your progress with these goals?

> **Attainable:** Are these goals achievable for you, and do you have the power to activate them? Explain.

> **Relevant:** Do these goals move you closer to reaching your greater vision? How?

> **Time Frame:** When do you want to achieve each goal.

Psychological Needs: Social & Esteem Needs

Now that we have developed an action plan for our basic needs, we can begin to review our psychological necessities, including our social and esteem needs. We can meet our social and esteem needs by learning how to use the belief cycle to our advantage. As you elevate your beliefs and thoughts, you will fulfill your psychological needs at these two levels.

Social Needs

As Maslow puts it, our social needs are made up of achieving a sense of belonging and acceptance with those around us. It is when we feel an abundance of love, appreciation, and gratitude for our existence. One may look at these requirements and assume that only external forces, people, and actions can fulfill this level of needs. This belief is a false perception handcuffing an individual into thinking that they have no control over meeting these necessities. Remember, how we are programmed influences how we see the world around us. Individuals who grow up in an unloving and unhealthy home will likely be programmed to believe that they are not worthy of love and acceptance regardless of the amount expressed by the outside world as they get older. If we genuinely want to meet our social needs, growing and developing our cognitive processes and elevating our external environments will be required. We must believe that we deserve love and belonging for them ever truly to become accomplished.

Acknowledge: Through your earlier self-assessments, take note if you are experiencing an inadequacy in meeting your needs for a healthy sense of belonging, acceptance, and love. Consider if the impact on these needs results from your external environment or your thought processes. Do you experience this lack in all settings or only in certain ones?

Assessment: Now that you know the source of your deficiencies regarding your social needs, you can now begin to identify the elevations you need to make to move towards the fulfillment of these needs. Complete the framework of the 6W questions to help in your assessment.

What is contributing to a lack of fulfillment of your social needs? Are the contributors an external cause from your environment, or are they a result of your thought processes? The nature of the root cause will differentiate whether you have to go to work on making internal or external changes. Again, it may be external if you feel negatively in specific spaces or with certain people. But it may be internal if your social needs suffering seems ever-present.

When did you first notice hindrances to these needs?

What does the ultimate fulfillment of these needs look like for you?

How can you begin to move towards fulfillment at this level of needs? In other words, what actions do you believe are necessary?

Why is it important for you to elevate and fulfill these needs? (Reflect upon your purpose and burning desires to help answer this question)

Where might you experience obstacles or roadblocks to fulfilling these needs? (Use Chapter 9 on *Overcoming Obstacles* to help answer this question)

Who might you need support from to make these changes?

Action: Through identifying your reasoning for a deprived sense of acceptance and belonging and understanding the changes you would like to apply to enhance these necessities, you will be able to create your plan of action for growth. Here are the questions to answer as you curate your plan of action. Remember, using the framework of SMART goals will provide you with clear, actionable steps to create lasting change successfully.

> **Specific:** What are your goals for fulfilling your social needs? These goals can be either internal focused, external focused, or both.

> **Measurable:** How will you track or measure your progress with these goals?

> **Attainable:** Are these goals obtainable for you, and do you have the power to activate them? Explain.

> **Relevant:** Do these goals move you closer to reaching your greater vision? How?

> **Time Frame:** When do you want to achieve each goal?

Esteem Needs

As you have discovered earlier in this book, an individual has two levels to their esteem needs. The lower level includes external validations and respect from others, while the higher level includes our self-beliefs, perceptions, worth, and confidence.

These two levels are intricately connected, both contributing to the health of an individual's overall esteem. Because of the relationship between the higher and lower esteem, we will aspire to construct a single blueprint for growth. It is also imperative that we recognize that this level of needs is linked to our cognitive processes; therefore, we must consider the significant influences on an individual's beliefs and thoughts as we develop this plan of action. Recall these four major impacts on our belief systems: Inner Dialogue, Stimulus & Energy Levels, Self-Esteem & Egotism, and Ignorance & Knowledge.

Acknowledge: Recognizing that the esteem level of needs relies upon the psychological complexes will be the key to your acknowledgment of the impacts of reaching healthy esteem. Take note if you are experiencing interference with meeting this level of needs due to your inner dialogue, energy levels, self-esteem & egotism, or the lack of knowledge regarding these needs. You may revisit the section describing esteem to help with your evaluations.

Assessment: During this review, it is paramount to understand the roots of these beliefs, thoughts, and emotions regarding why you are experiencing an inadequacy to this level of needs. Leaning on the previous chapters that have educated you on the belief cycle and the four influences on an individual's beliefs will be advantageous. Complete your review by contemplating the following thought-provoking questions.

What is contributing to a lack of fulfillment of your esteem needs? Consider the following:

- *Inner Dialogue:* Do you notice the presence of any negative self-speech or dialogue expressed towards yourself and or others? If you do, what are these negative thoughts?

- *Stimulus & Energy Levels:* Do you notice any energy leaks within your cognitive, physical or environmental energy zones? How do these energy leaks impact you?
- *Self-Esteem & Egotism:* What forms of ego are you expressing, and how are these egoic thoughts controlling you? Through letting down your walls and allowing vulnerability, ask yourself: what are the roots of these egotistical thoughts?
- *Ignorance & Knowledge:* What areas of your esteem needs do you lack knowledge and understanding? Perhaps it is a deficiency in awareness of the four impacts on your belief cycle? Are you open to learning and accepting new information?

When did you first notice hindrances to these needs?

What does the ultimate fulfillment of these needs look like for you? Identify your ideal outcome for each: Inner Dialogue, Stimulus & Energy Levels, Self-Esteem & Egotism, and Ignorance & Knowledge.

How can you begin to move towards fulfillment at this level of needs? In other words, what actions do you believe are necessary? Consider the following to help with this evaluation:

- *Inner Dialogue:* For those negative internal thoughts, what would be a positive dialogue you could use instead?

- *Stimulus & Energy Levels:* What is one thing you can do to eliminate the energy leak in each of your: cognitive, physical, or environmental energy zones?
- *Self-Esteem & Egotism:* How can you begin to shift these thoughts of egotism to that of a positive nature? What are the new beliefs you need to instill?
- *Ignorance & Knowledge:* What is one thing you can do to increase your understanding of the areas that impact your esteem needs?

Why is it important for you to elevate and fulfill these needs? (Reflect upon your purpose and burning desires to help answer this question)

Where might you experience obstacles or roadblocks to fulfilling each of these needs? (Use Chapter 9 on *Overcoming Obstacles* to help answer this question)

Who might you need support from to make these changes?

Action: Through identifying your reasoning for an unhealthy level of esteem and understanding the changes you would like to apply to enhance these necessities, you will be able to create your individualized plan of action. Here are some points to evaluate as you develop your game plan.

Specific: What are your goals for fulfilling your esteem needs? Consider setting one for each of the primary influences on these needs.

- *Inner Dialogue*
- *Stimulus & Energy Levels*
- *Self-Esteem & Egotism*
- *Ignorance & Knowledge*

Measurable: How will you track or measure your progress with these goals?

Attainable: Are these goals achievable for you, and do you have the power to activate them? Explain.

Relevant: Do these goals move you closer to reaching your greater vision? How?

Time Frame: When do you want to achieve each goal?

Self-Actualization Needs

By meeting our basic needs and developing our psychological needs, we create an environment conducive to growth and elevation. Here, we focus on pursuing greatness and living up to our full potential. Individuals at this level have an accurate perception of the world around them, with the openness to evolve their views as their knowledge grows. At this level of prosperity, problem-solving, radical transparency, and serving others are inherent traits of a self-actualized individual. Through developing your plan of action to move towards self-actualization, contemplate the below acknowledgments, assessments, and actions that may be necessary.

Acknowledge: This need for self-actualization is the yearning to achieve one's full and unique potential. Do you believe you are fulfilling your calling? An individual's ultimate purpose is composed of their burning desires, values, and vision. Have you taken the time to identify these?

Assessment: Knowing where you stand regarding the elements required for self-fulfillment will be foundational to revealing the changes you must make to reach your true potential. Consider the following 6W thought-provoking questions as you complete this assessment.

What is contributing to a lack of fulfillment of your self-actualization needs? Consider some of the following points as you make this assessment.

- Are your dreams indeed YOUR dreams? Or are they ideas planted by influential individuals in your life?
- Are you living through your values? Do you apply growth and development to all key pillars in your life?
- Do you make daily decisions based on educated thought processes? Or do you make emotional decisions that steer you off your path?
- Have you started the growth process, shifting from a fixed mindset to one of openness and growth? Are you open to new influence and information?
- Do you embrace the challenges that come your way as opportunities to grow and develop?
- Have you truly fulfilled the lower hierarchy of needs? With your intimate self-talk, energy levels, egotism, and ignorance, where are you at? These components can be the anchors holding you in place, preventing the growth you truly desire.

When did you first notice hindrances to these needs?

What does the ultimate fulfillment of these needs look like for you?

How can you begin to move towards fulfillment at this level of needs? In other words, what actions do you believe are necessary?

Why is it important for you to elevate and fulfill these needs? (Reflect upon your purpose and burning desires to help answer this question)

Where might you experience obstacles or roadblocks to fulfilling these needs? (Use Chapter 9 on *Overcoming Obstacles* to help answer this question)

Who might you need support from to make these changes?

Action: Assessing the foundational components required for achieving growth at this level of needs is necessary for revealing if you are on the path to living a purposeful life. Identifying the areas that are holding you back from reaching your true potential is the key to unlocking the changes and growth needed to achieve self-actualization.

Specific: What are your goals for fulfilling your self-actualization needs?

Measurable: How will you track or measure your progress with these goals?

Attainable: Are these goals achievable for you, and do you have the power to activate them? Explain.

Relevant: Do these goals move you closer to reaching your greater vision? How?

Time Frame: When do you want to achieve each goal?

Summary

Creating a plan to set sail on this incredible life journey is one of the critical steps to activating change. Transitioning from your lower self to your higher self will bring a significant amount of abundance, peace, and growth to your life, ultimately aligning you with your values and purpose. Remember, when you find yourself venturing off this path towards self-fulfillment, you can always find your way back by revisiting the six steps to activating lasting change. You will review your *Purpose Fueled by a Burning Desire, Take an Inventory, Take Ownership* of your past and present, and *Create a Plan and Take Action, Overcome Obstacles* superseded by *Review and Assess.* Through your consistency and determination, your elevation in all areas will also raise those around you. Recall that you can use the abundant universal energy flowing in all of us to help us succeed in all of our endeavors. Source is generous, expansive, unlimited, and creative. Because you are Source or God, you too have total abundance already within you. Now that you have a plan, and the action steps to implement, let's review potential obstacles you may encounter on your journey of elevation. Don't worry; I will walk you through the characteristics of these potential roadblocks and ways to overcome each obstruction as they may come up for you. Applying these teachings will ensure you have a supportive environment leading to the conditions for inevitable success.

"Obstacles don't have to stop you. If you run into a wall, don't turn around and give up. Figure out how to climb it, go through it, or work around it." ~ Michael Jordan

CHAPTER 9

Overcoming Obstacles & Reviewing Progress: Ensuring a Prosperous Environment

Creating a definitive plan followed by action must be supported by a magnitude of components. The last few chapters have covered the first four of the six steps to propel change in your life, which are necessary ingredients to developing a solid and straightforward blueprint for change. These first four steps include: identifying your *Purpose Fueled by a Burning Desire*, *Taking an Inventory* of your past and present, *Taking Ownership* of where you are in life, and *Creating a Plan and Taking Action*. Let's now look at the final two steps on your transformation journey: *Overcoming Obstacles* paired with *Review and Assess*.

Putting a plan into operation requires some critical supporting choices and behaviors that promote a healthy environment for change. Without these supportive actions, the journey of fostering growth can feel as if forces are working against you. An excellent analogy for this is to picture yourself pushing a heavy boulder up a mountain where you have the forces of gravity working against you. You may feel so overwhelmed thinking that this task is impossible to complete. You must keep pushing, never letting go of that boulder or gravity will take control, placing you back to the starting point or further down the mountain. Now, if you could use gravity to your advantage, imagine what it would be like rolling a boulder down a mountain. You have the force of gravity working in your favor, making this task much more manageable and even more enjoyable. You can take in the beautiful views and scenery as you make your way down the mountain. Creating a prosperous environment for growth and change is like the boulder analogy. You want to make sure the forces from your environment work with you rather than against you. You may not notice these forces pulling you back until you begin to move towards change. As you take steps forward, it is imperative to prioritize moments of pause to assess the direction and progress you are making. It is normal to veer off the path here and there, and when you do, it is the action of slowing down that brings clarity to the tweaks you must make to find your way back to the road that moves you toward your greater purpose. Let's look at some of the characteristics and assessments to complete using the 6W framework that we covered earlier and supporting actions to consider to establish the conditions for inevitable success.

Procrastination

Procrastination is a common hang-up for individuals working towards a goal. Those who struggle with this behavior think, "I'll do it later" or "I'm sure I can find time to do it tomorrow." They use this tactic to escape their realities, to waste their time on less important things. Procrastinators show limited to no decisiveness, leaving activities in limbo for long periods. Individuals who commonly think, "If I wait it out, hopefully, things will get better and turn out," will not progress on their self-fulfillment journey. If you do nothing, then nothing will happen. If you recall the boulder analogy, this unrealistic thinking is the same as if you thought, "if I just stand here in one spot, this rock will move itself." Here are some common character traits of those who procrastinate and suggestions to overcome these behaviors.

Characteristics of Procrastination

- **Procrastinators have a sense of distrust toward themselves**. If you keep saying you want to achieve something but keep putting things off, eventually, you will lose all trust in yourself to complete a task in the future. We can never build trust based on our promises; it can only be developed through our actions consistently over time.

- **There are different degrees of severity of procrastination.** There are moderate procrastinators who put things off until the last minute. These individuals justify their sloppy results on a "lack of time." And then there are the extreme procrastinators who put things off completely, making the excuse that they had no time.

- **Procrastination allows individuals to escape undesirable activities**. Frequently these individuals will provide reasons for avoiding growth and change while putting the responsibility onto others.

- **Procrastinators use distractions as their primary excuse for putting things off.** They will tell themselves, "I had other things to do" or "I was too busy." Some individuals will go as far as looking for these distractions to provide the excuses needed.

- **Individuals use procrastination as a layer of protection from failure and criticism.** This action allows an individual to shift responsibility from having to complete the task themselves to others. If things do not go well, they place the blame onto someone else's shoulders. If they never have to face the task, they can never fail.

Overcoming Procrastination

Acknowledge: Complete an open and honest self-evaluation about whether or not you recognize in yourself any of the above character traits regarding procrastination. Accepting the presence of this character trait is the first step to deactivating its power over you.

Assessment: Keeping in mind the procrastination traits identified above, evaluate the below questions as you may find them helpful if you desire to free yourself from this destructive behavior. The key here is to remain focused on the big picture. If you want to foster an environment supportive of your change, this is one of the many character traits you must go to work at eliminating.

> **What** procrastination traits are a part of your character?

> **When** did you first notice procrastination tendencies in your life? Consider evaluating your past and present.

What led to the manifestation of these traits in yourself? Take note of your beliefs, environments, and experiences to identify the cause of your delaying tendencies. Consider the following as you assess the roots of your procrastination.

- Do you recognize non-committal words within your current thoughts and expressions? Consider the following terms during your assessment: maybe, hopefully, possibly, potentially, or I wish.
- Do you recognize a lack of belief and trust in yourself to follow through on daily activities? Do you find yourself handing off responsibility for completing specific tasks to others?
- Do you recognize procrastinators within your upbringing or your current association?
- Do you have environments that promote laziness and hinder your follow-through?
- Do you fear failure? How do you view adversity, and how does it make you feel? Do you put off doing something when you fear failing at it?

What character traits are the opposite of procrastination?

How can you begin to move towards developing the character traits of action and follow through? In other words, what steps do you believe are necessary to overcome your procrastination?

Why is it essential for you to overcome these delaying tendencies of procrastination? (Reflect upon your mission statement, values, and burning desires to help answer this question)

Where might you experience obstacles or roadblocks as you shift from procrastination to action?

Who do you need to set boundaries with that may hold you back from becoming someone of action and follow-through?

Who might you need support from to make these changes?

Action: A detailed assessment will set the stage for success as you look to develop the habit of follow-through. Here are some powerful considerations as you elevate from procrastination to consistent action.

- **Accept ownership of your life.** This action means you must stop pushing off tasks or activities onto others and begin to own your decisions, including the actions you take. Only you can build your self-belief through action.
- **Set boundaries with individuals and limit your time investment.** You must choose to set healthy boundaries with those who hinder progression towards your goals. Limit your time spent with those who procrastinate and in specific settings that foster procrastination.
- **Accept that adversity and criticism will always be present no matter what you do.** Since the fear of failure is a common root of procrastination behavior, it is paramount that you begin to understand and accept that everyone receives disapproval through the journey of life. You must push past these lower energy beliefs and affirm that failure is a stepping stone to success.
- **Replace the non-committal words with those that stand firm in their commitment.** Consider phrases such as: "I

will," "I am," and "I can." This process is critical in the beginning to rewire the brain to manifest the character traits of follow-through. Since your inner beliefs lead to your outcomes, your bold statements of commitment will yield actions in alignment with this nature.

- **Rebuild broken trust with yourself by following through**. To rebuild the faith that you broke with yourself, you must begin the process of following through. Start by making a small prioritized list of what you would like to achieve. Begin to schedule small time blocks into your calendar to complete these tasks. The key here is to ensure you follow through on these commitments. The more you follow through, the more you begin to build self-trust.
- **Create an environment that is supportive of change.** As you make the bold decision to eradicate procrastination from your life, your environment must support this change. As you follow through on tasks you have scheduled for yourself, eliminate all distractions, including electronics, apps, people, animals, noises, activities, and anything else that will take your focus away from the task at hand.

Fear of Failure

Our society breeds an environment where failure, adversity, and challenges are viewed as something negative. The education system is a significant contributor to this thought process, where students are mentally programmed to believe that failure is bad. As you experience D's and F's, soon you will be labeled as someone who is intellectually inadequate because you have failed a grade, all the while disappointing your parents. This label can stay with you for a lifetime, limiting your beliefs and actions as you hope that you won't have to experience the pain of failure again. This negative thought process of failure results in fears manifesting, leading to lower energy vibrations and adverse outcomes. As you embark on your growth journey, the fear of failure is one of the most common hindrances to success. To break free from this loop, let's look at the characteristics of failure and suggestions to elevate your thoughts.

Characteristics of the Fear of Failure

- **They lack a clear vision of what they desire for themselves.** Individuals paralyzed by their fears of failure have allowed themselves to become trapped in a state of scarcity fueled by their thoughts of "what if." They are more focused on surviving vs. thriving, which steals their ability to create a vision for the future.
- **Individuals who fear failure have very little determination to aim high.** Their fears of the possible adverse outcomes persuade them to avoid challenges that promote growth, leaving them stuck in their current situations.
- **The fear of failure leads to avoidance of change with the hopes of getting good at one thing.** They believe that "if I don't change and continue to do what I am good at, there will be less failure." They live their lives on repeat, doing the same thing every day.
- **Lacking self-discipline and giving up too quickly when faced with adversity.** When things get too complicated, or there are no immediate solutions, individuals who fear failure will give up quickly, giving into their lower self. They think the answer to adversity is quitting.
- **Indecision and procrastination are common side effects of this debilitating fear.** Those who have experienced significant hardships in their past and chose not to overcome them may have analysis paralysis. They

have allowed their fears induced by past circumstances to hinder their current decision-making abilities.

Overcoming the Fear of Failure

Acknowledge: As you have read some of the prevalent character traits for those who experience the fear of failure, take the time to reflect upon your own beliefs, thoughts, and emotions around adversity and challenges. Do you notice any of the above character traits present in your life?

Assessment: In reviewing how you handle failure, if you diagnose the existence of negative thoughts and emotions around experiencing it, perhaps you may struggle with this fear. It is paramount to identify the causes of these negative beliefs if you wish to use adversity as a motivator rather than a paralyzer.

> **What** traits regarding the fear of failure do you recognize in yourself?

> **When** did you first notice these fears in your life? Consider evaluating your past and present to understand where your fear of failure began.

> **What** led to the manifestation of these traits in yourself? Take note of your beliefs, thoughts, environments, and experiences to identify the cause of these fears. Consider the following as you complete your assessment.

> • Assess your thoughts and beliefs around failure. How do you view yourself as you walk through challenging or unsuccessful moments? Do you

experience negative self-talk? What phrases go through your mind as you experience failure?

- Evaluate your level of self-belief and confidence. Do you believe you can handle challenging tasks, or do your fears paralyze you? Are your aspirations left unfulfilled because of this?
- Was there a moment, event, or outcome that triggered this fear for you?
- Were you disciplined through moments of adversity, or were you encouraged through them?
- Contemplate your inputs and the environments you participate in. Is it toxic, full of ego and comparison? Or are you surrounded by uplifting and encouraging individuals?

What character traits are the opposite of those of someone who fears failure? Consider the words of having the courage to face adversity.

How can you begin to embody the courage to face adversity? In other words, what actions do you believe are necessary to overcome your fear of failure?

Why is it vital for you to overcome the fear of failure? (Reflect upon your mission statement, values, and burning desires to help answer this question)

Where might you experience obstacles or roadblocks as you develop the character traits in line with having the courage to face failure?

Who do you need to set boundaries with that may hold you back from becoming someone courageous to act and face their fear of failure?

Who might you need support from to make these changes?

Action: By assessing your fears regarding failure, you are equipped to put some of the below recommendations into action. These are only a few of the many things you can do to elevate these negative emotions.

- **Evaluate your past and present.** Understanding where your fear of failure began will be paramount in clarifying how you got to where you are. Using the assessment questions provided earlier will help you with this evaluation.
- **Rewire your thought process around failure and its role in creating abundance.** You must stop seeing failure or adversity as a bad thing. Each time an outcome does not happen the way you thought it would, reframe your thoughts to view it as a positive outcome. You can do this by understanding that you have opened up the opportunity to learn and discover what will work when something does not work. If you do not try and fail, you will never grow. During each challenging moment or season, consider asking yourself, what am I to learn at this moment?
- **Accept that adversity and criticism will always be present no matter what you do.** You must begin to understand that there will always be criticisms, challenges, and even failure present with everything you do. Begin to affirm that failure is a stepping stone to success, and without it, you are not moving forward.

- **Replace the fear-inducing words with those that build up the courage.** Consider shifting from "what if" to phrases such as "I will," "I am," and "I can." This process is critical in rewiring the brain, moving from a fearful and fixed mindset to one that is open and growing.
- **Set boundaries with individuals and limit your time investment.** Choose to restrict the time spent with individuals who criticize the failures or adversities you face. Set boundaries with yourself when participating in settings that trigger your fears.

Lacking Persistence

Persistence is the continuous efforts by someone or something to continue moving forward with a goal regardless of the outcomes. When you combine your burning desires with willpower, you create a force that is so powerful it cannot be stopped. This drive is persistence. As you begin to elevate yourself to higher frequency thoughts, vibrations and actions, you will not see results immediately. You will be working hard and making changes for some time before you begin to see your best self and your dream life coming to fruition. Because of this, individuals searching for instant gratification can easily slip into self-sabotage if they lack this key ingredient, the persistence of resiliency. Those that lack this character trait are considered quitters, lazy, lethargic, and lacking tenacity. Let's look at how this trait operates and how to develop it as part of your character.

Characteristics of Lacking Persistence

- **They do not have a clear vision of what they desire for themselves.** Individuals who lack the character trait of persistence or follow-through have allowed laziness into their life. These individuals will not prioritize the time and apply the work necessary to develop a rooted and value-based vision.

- **Lacking the tenacity to go after what you want is a habitual trait.** Since habits form through thought, one can infer that minimal drive for fulfillment is self-induced by our programmed minds. Experience from an individual's past, inner dialogue, energy levels, and esteem all contribute to these beliefs and thoughts tied to inaction.

- **Individuals known as "quitters" struggle to follow through on commitments made**. They may say they will do something and then lack the ability to follow through. You will not succeed if laziness and inaction are a part of your default programming. This quitting mentality is one of the major causes of undesirable outcomes.

- **These individuals tend to choose comfort overgrowth.** Although we all have our comfort zones, the difference between someone who has the tenacity and those that don't is the amount of time individuals choose to spend in their comfort zones. A tenacious person will spend very little time bounded by their comforts, and those that lack ambition spends most, if not all, of their time in this zone. Stepping out into the unknown is required if you want to live a more extraordinary life.

- **Cutting corners and taking shortcuts is a way of life for lazy individuals.** If you do not have persistence as you pursue greatness, you will look to cut corners, provide excuses when things do not turn out, and quit moving forward. You will not complete things with the highest quality possible.

Developing Persistence

Acknowledge: Having a limited amount of determination to persevere through uncomfortable or challenging times indicates lacking persistence. Through your evaluations of these characteristics above, take note of those negatively influencing your life.

Assessment: Through fearlessly accepting your lack of persistence, you are equipped, through your vulnerability, to assess the cause of this behavior. Here are some suggestions as you complete your assessment.

> **What** traits regarding the lack of persistence do you recognize in yourself?

> **When** did these character traits begin to be expressed? Consider evaluating your past and present to understand your lack of persistence.

> **What** led to the manifestation of these traits in yourself? Take note of your beliefs, thoughts, environments, and experiences to identify the cause of lacking persistence. Consider the following as you complete your assessment.

> > • Take time to review your inner beliefs and thoughts. Do you recognize the presence of any lower energy thoughts and emotions that support the habits of laziness or quitting?
> > • Evaluate your values and vision. Do you know what you stand for with a clear vision for your future? Or do you have a blurred vision, unsure of the direction you would like to move?

- What are the outcomes you are experiencing in your life? Do you notice a significant number of undesirable results? Did you push through these moments of adversity, or did you quit?
- Assess your environments and associations. Do individuals in your association aid in your habits of laziness and quitting? Do you participate in environments that support these habits? Were you often allowed to give up when you found something difficult as a child?
- As you move forward with challenging tasks, do you look to cut corners with the hopes of shortening the process? Do you find yourself choosing comfort overgrowth?

What character traits are the opposite of those of someone who lacks persistence? Consider the words: tenacious, persistent, stamina, and endurance.

How can you begin to embody the character traits of persistence? In other words, what actions do you believe are necessary to overcome your lazy or quitting ways?

Why is it paramount to overcome the lack of persistence? (Reflect upon your mission statement, values, and burning desires to help answer this question)

Where might you experience obstacles or roadblocks as you develop the character traits of tenacity and persistence?

Who do you need to set boundaries with that may hold you back from becoming someone who is tenacious?

Who might you need support from to make these changes?

Action: When you are ready to activate change in your life, moving from inaction to perseverance, assess the suggestions below to help with this transformation journey.

- **Develop an awareness of and accept ownership of your lazy or quitting tendencies.** These actions require you to become vulnerable as you recognize and accept the presence of laziness. Only through awareness can you transform these negative habits into those of a positive nature.
- **Create an indestructible vision so powerful that it fuels you into action.** To activate unwavering progression towards a purpose, you must have a motivation that runs deep inside. If you struggle with persistence, review your mission statement, and ask yourself, "does my desire for change outweigh the pain of staying the same?"
- **Rewire your brain to foster tenacious habits.** As you may have noticed with other character traits, replacing non-committal words with those that stand firm in their commitment is essential for all areas of your personal growth. Again, use phrases such as: "I will," "I am," and "I can" to begin to rewrite the narratives you may have told yourself. This process is critical in the beginning to rewire the brain to manifest the character traits of commitment and follow-through, including during adverse times. By simply telling yourself that you can do something, you will become better equipped to follow through.

- **Accept adversities and challenges as the answer to building up this character trait.** Only through difficult moments can you develop the character trait of persistence. It is easy to follow through when things are going well; during the challenging times, your actual level of commitment will be revealed, tested, and strengthened. Continuously remind yourself that failure is a requirement to build up your persistence, and persistence would not be persistence if you didn't persist through difficulty.
- **Set boundaries with individuals and time.** Choose to limit the time spent with individuals that lack persistence and tenacity. Their habits of inaction can and will continue to influence you. Prioritize time with those that inspire and motivate you to follow through.
- **Create an environment that is supportive of change.** As you build up the character trait of persistence, eliminate all distractions that can pull you back into a state of laziness and inactivity. These distractions include electronics, apps, people, animals, noises, activities, etc. Consider using tools such as: hiring a babysitter, changing your environment when you want to focus on a task, and eliminating technology distractions to foster an environment conducive to change.
- **Break free from the comfort zone into the ever-expanding growth zone**. To move into a state of persistence, build your momentum with small wins that can push you outside of your comfort zone. Choose to participate in one small thing at a time that will stretch you beyond your comfort. Maintain your momentum by continuing to step into the uncomfortable and unknown, maybe a little more or more often. The more you step outside of the chains of comfort, the more you begin to build new habits of action, tenacity, and persistence. The

stronger these habits become, the more you can withstand challenging times.

Approval Seeking

It is normal and healthy to appreciate others' accolades, compliments, and acknowledgments. These positive affirmations from others can lead to raising your own personal energy levels, creating a positive environment for creating success. Issues arise when we develop the need for approval from others, handing over decision-making into their hands. By giving away the control of your life, you are also giving away the outcomes you desire. Your personal truths, confidence, and authenticity disappear in the hopes of meshing who you are with those around you. Those that stand for everything stand for nothing. In other words, by seeking only the acceptance of others, you will never discover what you truly desire yourself. If you recognize your need for the approval of others before you implement new changes in your life, you must break free of this detrimental habit. Once you accomplish complete freedom from people-pleasing tendencies, you will step into that version of you that is living in alignment to your authentic desires. Let's look at the traits of people-pleasing tendencies and how you can make your own stand.

Characteristics of Approval Seeking

- **They lack firm values and a clear vision of their desire for themselves.** These individuals usually have a distorted values system and a vision composed of what others want for them to appease others. They put aside their true innate desires to satisfy others. Without definitive values, one will become lost, feeling as if they are living someone else's life

- **They lack confidence and faith in their decision-making.** Those who become immobilized by the opinions of others experience paralysis in their ability to make decisive decisions. Flip-flopping becomes an inherent trait of people pleasers to make others happy. When you've made decisions to appease others, you have slowly destroyed any trust you may have had with yourself over time.

- **Approval seekers are sensitive to being questioned and criticized**. They take things personally, which results in high emotional states. They blame others for their emotional outbursts because they can't fathom taking responsibility for their own emotions.

- **These individuals have poor boundary-setting skills with an inability to say no.** They would rather sacrifice their fulfillment to make others happy. This decision leaves them feeling exhausted, overworked, and underappreciated. The energy leaks from this behavior result in limited to no energy left for these individuals to apply towards themselves. You must plug the drain to fill your energy tank.

Overcoming Approval Seeking

As one looks to break through the bounds of pleasing others, remember that your goal here is to begin to live the life you desire, free from the need to please others. As you take these steps forward, here are some tips to help you take action.

Acknowledge: During your review of the many characteristics of approval seeking, it is important that you are sincere and candid with your evaluations. It takes courage to admit when you have given up control of your life to those around you. This courage will aid you in snipping the strings that have influenced your every move. With your willingness to be vulnerable, make a list of your people-pleasing and approval-seeking impulses.

Assessment: Through your vulnerability, you will be able to move past the acknowledgments stage into a more profound evaluation. Be patient and kind with yourself, as this evaluation can stir up emotions of frustration and disapproval.

What approval-seeking character traits do you see present in yourself?

When did these character traits begin to be expressed? Consider evaluating your past and present to understand where your people-pleasing and need for acceptance came from.

What led to the manifestation of approval seeking within yourself? Take note of your beliefs, thoughts, environments, and experiences to identify the cause. Consider the following as you complete your assessment.

- Review your values, vision, and purpose. Determine if they are authentically yours or made up of someone else's. Do you have a clear view of the direction you are headed, or do you feel lost or stuck when not receiving the advice and feedback of others?
- An individual's need for acceptance and approval is a habit that has formed over time. Since all habits result from the belief cycle, you must evaluate the roots of your stored thoughts and feelings towards appeasing others. What are your

thoughts and feelings when you face opposition? If applicable, why is it vital for you to change your innate beliefs to make others happy?

- Review your past and present to understand the environments, associations, and inputs that may be impacting your cognitive processes. Do you recall painful moments of being judged, criticized, and rejected? Do you struggle with saying no to others because of this?

- If you recognize sensitivities and negative emotions to people criticizing or providing feedback, take the time to identify why. Do these emotions serve or hinder your decision-making?

What character traits represent those that are free from approval seeking?

How can you begin to overcome your people-pleasing ways? In other words, what actions do you believe are necessary to be free from approval seeking?

Why is it essential for you to overcome approval seeking? (Reflect upon your mission statement, values, and burning desires to help answer this question)

Where might you experience obstacles or roadblocks as you develop character traits that are independent and free from others' opinions?

Who do you need to set boundaries with that may hold you back from developing this independence?

Who might you need support from to make these changes?

Action: Understanding your cognitive programming around approval seeking and identifying the root causes is a great place to start with eradicating these limitations we place upon ourselves. As you begin to take action towards living a life solely designed for you, here are some suggestions to help streamline this process.

- **Develop your own unwavering vision and values.** Take time to identify your core beliefs and values and become firmly rooted in them so that no one can shake your tree. You must stop giving power to outside forces to control your thoughts, feelings, actions, and destiny. Take responsibility for your life. What do you truly want?
- **Rewire your thought process and learn to accept criticism.** Recognize that everyone receives disapproval through the journey of life. It is essential to acknowledge that this has nothing to do with who you are and what you stand for. You must develop emotional stability in moments of judgment to make clear and educated decisions. Stay focused on your vision, and the criticisms from others will bounce right off you.
- **Replace people-pleasing thoughts with those that stand firm in self-fulfillment.** Consider phrases such as: "I will," "I am," and "I can." This process is critical in forming the independent charter traits needed to overcome people-pleasing. This self-speech includes: "I will make my own decisions," "I am capable of saying no to others," or "I will move forward regardless of the judgments or criticisms I receive." This reprogramming feeds the mind with self-belief and encouragement while eradicating the thoughts of fear and discouragement.

- **Set boundaries with individuals and get comfortable saying "no."** Choose to set boundaries and limit the time spent with individuals that do not support your stand for independence. You must also set boundaries with yourself when you're participating in settings that trigger your approval-seeking tendencies.
- **Look for inspiration by reviewing the triumphs of great leaders from our past who endured a significant amount of criticism and judgment.** Such leaders include; Albert Einstein, Henry Ford, Orville and Wilbur Wright, Steve Jobs, Thomas Edison, Martin Luther King Jr, and many more. What did they all have in common? They endured through the judgments of others to achieve monumental outcomes. A quote by Wayne Dyer reveals that "those who seem to get the most approval in life are those who never seek it out." [1] This implies that a by-product of independence and being free from the need to please others will result in true acceptance.

Dependency

The need for something or someone in your life to help support you emotionally, psychologically, and physically is a sign of dependency. If you find yourself frozen from action because you need support from key individuals in your life, you have handed over the reins to someone outside of yourself. What happens if these individuals you rely on disappear? Without self-control, much like people-pleasing, this character trait eliminates your uniqueness with diminishing confidence and authenticity. Dependency differs from people-pleasing because you are not looking for general approval but are reliant on specific individuals, such as a romantic partner, a parent, or a friend, without whom you feel as if you cannot function or feel fulfilled. With the desire for growth and change, it is necessary to overcome the dependency you have adopted to create a prosperous life that is true to yourself. It is OK and healthy to want and need things from others but not depend on them entirely. Through understanding the nature of dependency, you can free yourself from the chains holding you back from ultimate freedom.

Dependency Character Traits

- **Those who are dependent typically lack self-reliance and are controlled by something or someone.** Let's consider the principle that "you are treated how you teach others to treat you." With your dependency behavior, you have taught people to dominate and control your life. You have shown them that you need them to lead the way.
- **Individuals with a dependency nature will have a blurred vision infused with the ideas of those that they depend upon.** They usually have a wavering values system and a vision that is distorted. This indistinctiveness is because they attempt to mesh other individuals' values and vision with their own or completely adopt another's values and vision. They put aside their true innate desires to achieve comfort in knowing that they are moving in the same direction as those they rely on. Without individualized values, one will become lost because they attempt to live someone else's life.
- **Psychological dependency is when your thoughts and emotions are dependent on the thoughts and feelings of others**. Suppose someone you depend upon expresses negative cognitive processes with high emotional states. In that case, you, too, will express these thoughts and emotions as you are simply an extension of the one you rely on.

- **Physical dependency is relying on others to support you financially and physically.** By choosing to be physically dependent upon others, you rob yourself of experiencing true independence and freedom. A great example is a 30-year-old still living at home; they rely on their parents to physically put a roof over their head and financially put food on the table.
- **Those reliant on others tend to avoid responsibility for their behavior and outcomes.** They blame their mistakes on others, avoid hard work and escape making essential decisions. Consider the ways of a dependent newborn child and their need for full-time support. What is the difference between a newborn child and a dependent adult? The appearance of their physique, nothing more.
- **A typical root for dependency is a lack of confidence, experience, and knowledge in a particular area.** There is a difference between a dependent and a student. A student learns from the wisdom of others and applies it in their life to evolve. A dependent does not take the necessary steps for growth; they choose to remain stagnant in their life and continue to rely on others for their knowledge and experiences.

Eliminating Dependency

Acknowledge: The first step to independence is recognizing if you have dependent tendencies. Do you notice any of the above characteristics present in your life?

Assessment: Recognizing your dependent and needy nature is a decisive moment of courage within yourself. Many individuals think that if they choose dependency, it makes their life better, so they avoid taking responsibility. However, they don't realize that they allow others to dictate their lives and the outcomes that transpire. Here are some things to consider as you evaluate the reliance tendencies in your life.

What dependency character traits do you see present in yourself?

When did these character traits begin to be expressed? Consider evaluating your past and present to understand when your reliance on others started.

What led to the dependency character traits you have acquired? Take note of your beliefs, thoughts, environments, and experiences to identify the cause. Consider the following as you complete your assessment.

- Assess your mission statement and values making up your key pillars. Are they made up of what you want for yourself, or do they include the vision, values, and desires of what others want? Do you know what you want, or are all of your desires intertwined with others?
- This dependency nature is a habitual thought process where you believe you need someone or something to survive or thrive. Assess your psychological belief cycle to identify the thoughts and emotions you have regarding this behavior. Do you believe that you would not survive without the person or thing that you rely on?
- Evaluating your physical situation, do you believe you need support financially or physically? Why

do you need this support? What would happen if you no longer had this physical backing?

- Through assessing your behavior, do you notice a lack in stepping up and taking responsibility for your actions and results in your life? If so, what do you believe the root cause is?
- Having limited knowledge in a specific area is normal; what do you do when encountering these situations? Do you seek to understand and apply? Or do you find someone you can lean on for all your questions without applying the growth to yourself?

What character traits represent those that are independent of others?

How can you begin to overcome your dependency nature? In other words, what actions do you believe are necessary to be independent?

Why is it vital for you to overcome dependency? (Reflect upon your mission statement, values, and burning desires to help answer this question)

Where might you experience obstacles or roadblocks as you develop character traits independent from others?

Who do you need to set boundaries with that may hold you back from developing this independence?

Who might you need support from to make these changes?

Action: As you choose to cut the umbilical cords of dependency, you take one of the required courageous steps forward to live an independent and thriving life. To support this severance, here are some actions to consider.

- **Develop your own unwavering mission statement supported by your key value pillars.** Take time to identify your core beliefs and values that are genuinely independent of the values of those around you. You must separate what other individuals want for themselves from your vision.

- **Declare your intention of achieving psychological sovereignty, which is the total freedom mentally and emotionally from relationships around you.** This autonomy requires the elimination of external behaviors controlling your life. You must become psychologically self-directed, moving confidently in the direction of your ultimate purpose. As you control your own thoughts and emotions, you will shift towards independence and self-reliance.

- **Create a plan and work towards complete physical independence.** This form of self-reliance means being financially independent of those around you and those who have supported you. To achieve financial accountability, make it known that you intend to be supporting yourself. To achieve this outcome, you must stop accepting handouts for your cell phone bill, car payments, rent, and any other bills you are responsible for. When things get tough, you must apply your persistence to elevate through the situation.

- **Replace dependent words and phrases with those standing firm in their independence.** Consider terms such as: "I will," "I am," and "I can." This process is critical in forming the independent beliefs and character traits needed to overcome dependency. Implement the self-speech of: "I will make my own decisions" or "I am capable of saying no." Here you will begin to rewire your mental complexes of reliance, and you will begin to instill thoughts rooted in autonomy.

- **Set firm boundaries with your association and environments.** Choosing independence will require implementing limits with yourself and others to ensure that you participate in settings that do not trigger your dependency behaviors. Become comfortable saying "no" to the people and things that over-step your choice for self-reliance. Prioritize relationships that support and encourage your autonomy. If you are dependent on someone, they may also be dependent on you. It may be challenging to untangle the dependency of the relationship; however, you will have to face this to foster your independence.

- **Choose to apply the knowledge gained**. Learning from or asking others for something is OK, as long as the individual takes the information they are receiving and uses it for their own growth and knowledge. It is important to be independent and self-sufficient on the information gathering journey; consider putting your own efforts into reading, audio, and other means of self-learning.

Summary

By acknowledging, assessing, and taking action on any of the perceived roadblocks in your life, you will be better primed to become the best version of yourself. Creating an environment fertile for change and prosperity is essential for the lifelong journey of success and happiness. It is necessary to know in your mind and heart that you have control of your environment and can make alterations at any time. During those wandering moments where you find yourself veering off the path to your purpose due to obstructions, remember that you can eliminate all obstacles you face. An environment full of action, growth, determination, responsibility, independence, and accountability will create a smooth journey back to your destined path. You must accept that there is no such thing as perfection; it is all about progression.

"You may have lost your way more than a little bit, but I believe you can find your way back. That's the trick. Finding your way back." ~ Eleanor Brown

CHAPTER 10

Applying the Six Critical Steps to Change

In the beginning pages of this book, I've shared my personal growth journey with you, which coincided with the beginning of the COVID-19 pandemic. All of the transformational work I committed to leading up to the pandemic was foundational in helping me face the challenging times that were to come. Yes, I slipped back to old ways of thinking for some time; however, I was well equipped to make my way back to the path towards self-actualization because of the tools I'm sharing with you now. The knowledge I had gained during the years prior was, without a doubt, my saving grace. I wholeheartedly believe my family would have been significantly worse off had we not built the foundation of growth that we did before entering such a difficult time. It is never too late in your life to begin this journey of enlightenment, and there is no better time than now to start living the life you truly desire.

As part of my effort to help others utilize the six steps to activating lasting change, I will share my intimate process of applying them during the Coronavirus pandemic as a case study. In the early chapters of this book, you have learned about my first step, *Purpose Fueled by a Burning Desire*. Additionally, I touched on Step 2, *Taking an Inventory of my Past*, leading up to the pandemic. To continue Step 2, in this chapter, I will *Take an Inventory of my Present*, which at the time is during COVID-19. Additionally, I will show you how I applied Step 3: *Taking Ownership, Step 4: Creating a Plan and Taking Action*, and Step 5: *Overcoming Obstacles*. The following chapter will detail the fulfillment of Step 6, *Review and Assess*.

To clarify the areas that required growth, I will use Maslow's five levels of needs: physiological needs, safety needs, social needs, esteem needs, and self-actualization. To show how I applied the six steps to activating change at each level, I will use the three A's: *acknowledge, assessment and action*. Let's review this framework here:

- *Acknowledgment* is the identification phase where you begin to fulfill Step 2, *Taking an Inventory*.
- *Assessment* is the evaluation completed where you continue to add to Step 2, *Taking an Inventory*, in combination with fulfilling Step 3, *Taking Ownership*. Here I will use the successful coaching technique, the 6W framework, to dive deep into my assessment.
- *Action* is the process required to reach your goals. Here I will fulfill Step 4, *Creating a Plan and Taking Action*. Additionally, I will begin to touch on Step 5, *Overcoming Obstacles*. I will use the SMART goal methodology to establish the effective actions required.

I will continue to offer my story and intimate thoughts experienced during this difficult time with the hopes of providing a real-world example, helping you to see how this work can be implemented in your life today, even through a difficult time like a pandemic. I also recognize that if I want to truly help you see the depth of honesty required during your self-reflections, I need to be vulnerable and transparent with you. You may notice that I share parts of my intimate journey of elevation using the present tense; this is to magnify your experience of what it looks like to assess and begin to take action when you are experiencing it. As you continue to read on, in no way am I here to convince anyone of the direction or path they should take; my transparency is meant to serve one purpose only, to help you become vulnerable with yourself. I hope you can approach these pages with the same mindset and attitude. I also encourage you to complete your self-assessment to truly take advantage of this opportunity to understand precisely where you are. Mastering any judgments, criticisms, or assumptions you may experience will allow you to open up to your higher self. This action of dismissing these negative thoughts is a great way to practice letting go of your dominating ego and taking control of your thoughts and emotions.

Basic Needs: Physiological & Safety Needs

After taking the time to analyze my basic needs, both physical and safety, during this time of COVID-19, it was very revealing that a lot of my concerns were fueled by fears paired with negative thoughts. The actual threat to my basic needs was not as severe as my mind made them out to be. My physiological and safety needs were not, in reality, being compromised significantly. I had formed a "truth" based on the information available to me and based on emotion: fear. My thoughts were very toxic and operating on a low frequency, allowing me to give in to this fear. You will learn more about how I elevated my thoughts to a higher frequency later in this chapter under; Psychological Needs. Going back to my basic needs, I will share my acknowledgments, assessments, and actions to help fulfill these lower-level necessities to build a strong foundation for the subsequent stages of growth.

Physiological Needs

Acknowledge: My family and I were incredibly fortunate to have a limited impact on our basic physical needs throughout the pandemic. The necessities that were experiencing strain included the need for sleep and my physical health.

Assessment: Knowing the specific areas of my basic needs that were being threatened, the next step was to dive deep into my evaluation to understand more about these hinderances. Using the 6W framework, here is an in-depth assessment of my physiological needs affected throughout COVID-19.

> **What** is contributing to a lack of fulfillment of your physiological needs?
>
> *Sleep:* Lack of sleep due to anxieties experienced.
>
> *Anxiety:* My fears began as a pandemic status was declared and continued throughout the different phases of COVID-19, including the vaccination roll-out stage.
>
> *Physical Health:* Physical health declined due to a significant amount of stress in my life coupled with gym closure for a couple of months.

When did you first notice hindrances to these needs?

> *Sleep:* Reduced sleep began when the World Health Organization declared that the globe had entered a pandemic.

> *Anxiety:* My anxious state began as COVID-19 spread to Canada, resulting in the shutdown of our nation.

> *Physical Health:* Physical health declined due to a significant amount of stress in my life and the closing of wellness centers within the first few months.

What does the ultimate fulfillment of these needs look like for you?

> *Sleep:* Fulfilling my need for sleep and rest would involve getting a full seven-hour sleep without disrupting necessary sleep cycles.

> *Anxiety:* Becoming free from concerns and worries would mean that I have achieved peace and contentment within my psychological processes. My thoughts would be those full of positivity, love, and abundance.

> *Physical Health:* Fulfilling my physical health involves a consistent movement and exercise regime while eliminating stress.

How can you begin to move towards fulfillment at this level of needs? In other words, what actions do you believe are necessary?

Sleep: To achieve a healthy level of sleep and rest, I need to work on my anxieties spurred by COVID-19 and implement a new sleeping routine to increase the hours of rest achieved.

Anxiety: I could consider talking to an anxiety coach, reading resources, or listening to audiobooks and podcasts.

Physical Health: To improve my physical health, I could set up the necessary equipment at home and develop a new exercise regime involving strength building, toning, and stretching. I could consider additional resources such as YouTube videos for yoga, pilates, and kickboxing.

Why is it essential for you to elevate and fulfill these needs? (Reflect upon your purpose and burning desires to help answer this question)

Improving my sleep, anxiety, and physical health is vital to ensure I have the energy to fulfill the other key pillars of my life, such as my faith, relationships, finances, and calling.

Where might you experience obstacles or roadblocks to fulfilling these needs? (Use Chapter 9 on *Overcoming Obstacles* to help answer this question)

Sleep: Potential obstructions to fulfilling my need for sleep includes the possibility of continued anxieties and external influences out of my control, such as my kids waking up throughout the night.

Anxiety: A possible hindrance to overcoming my worries is having a lack of persistence to work through my paralyzing concerns.

Physical Health: Potential obstacles to elevating my physical health include a lack of perseverance to follow through with an exercise regime at home.

Who might you need support from to make these changes?

Sleep: To help fulfill my need for sleep, I would need my husband's engagement to take on some of the responsibilities with the kids.

Anxiety: Additionally, I could use the support of a coach for guidance on my anxiety.

Physical Health: To improve my health, I would need to enlist my husband's support to watch the kids while I worked out.

Actions: Through completing my review and identifying the hindrances to these needs, I established some SMART goals outlining the steps necessary to begin the process of growth.

Specific: What are your goals for fulfilling your Physiological Needs?

Sleep: My first goal in fulfilling my physiological needs is to improve my sleep, which will require my husband's time and support to watch the kids for extra moments of rest.

Anxiety: My second goal is to work on my anxieties consciously by enlisting the help of an anxiety coach.

Physical Health: My third goal involves setting up a home gym and establishing a new workout routine, including weight training, kickboxing, pilates, running, and yoga. I will commit to 45-minute workouts five days a week.

Measurable: How will you track or measure your progress with each goal?

Sleep: For sleep, I will set a boundary to be in bed at 10 pm every night.

Anxiety: For anxiety, I will time block an hour to meet with my coach on the same day every week: Tuesdays at 8 pm.

Physical Health: I will track this goal by adding it to my daily tracker for exercise and movement.

Attainable: Is each goal achievable for you, and do you have the power to activate them? Explain.

Yes, each of these goals is attainable and within my control. They will require my commitment to follow through and are independent of relying on external circumstances to be achieved.

Relevant: Do these goals move you closer to reaching your greater vision? How?

As I fulfill these goals, I will strengthen my health pillar while meeting my basic needs. By solidifying my physiological necessities, I will create a foundation that will enable me to move towards and elevate the second level within my hierarchy of needs: safety.

Time Frame: When do you want to achieve each goal?

Sleep: I will get seven hours of sleep every night after one month of going to bed at 10 pm.

Anxiety: I will begin overcoming my fears after three months of working with my anxiety coach every Tuesday at 8 pm.

Physical Health: I will reach elevated physical health within three months of committing to 45-minute workouts five days a week.

Safety Needs

With the outbreak of the unknown Coronavirus and the closing of our nations, it makes sense that the resulting consequence was a threat to humanity's safety, including my very own. My physical and economic safety needs became vulnerable, having an enormous impact on my sense of security.

Physical Safety Needs

Acknowledge: Due to the various stages throughout the pandemic, I experienced different threats to my physical safety. Initially, I feared the mysterious Coronavirus, and subsequently, as things progressed, I developed a fear of the vaccine. At one point each of these components was an actual threat to my safety needs, however, over time they shifted from a threat to just a fear.

Assessment: After experiencing threats to my physical security, I knew that I needed to understand these negative impacts deeper. Here is a review of my commitment to vulnerably open and share my inner evaluations while using the 6W sequence of questions.

What is contributing to a lack of fulfillment of your physical safety needs? Consider your personal engagements, surrounding environments, associations, and your job.

Coronavirus: Initially, I had paralyzing fears of the unknown Coronavirus that swept our nations. With limited data on the health risks associated with the virus, my worries became exasperated.

Vaccines: Later, I had concerns about the safety of experimental vaccines, and I had extreme hesitancies due to the political pressure to roll out a vaccine as quickly as possible. I also found it incredibly concerning that there was a lack of transparency on the safety and efficacy of the vaccines as the government chose to censor the experts, doctors, and scientists. Furthermore, I started noticing the side effects of the COVID injections leading to a fear of receiving the vaccine.

When did you first notice hindrances to these needs?

Coronavirus: The day the globe entered a pandemic status was when my fears of the Coronavirus appeared.

Vaccines: My concerns about the vaccine arose as governments began to rush the science required to fully evaluate these inoculations' safety and effectiveness.

What does ultimate fulfillment of your physical safety needs look like? Describe the environment in which you would be safe.

I cannot control the presence of COVID-19 nor the rollout of vaccines. However, I can enhance my awareness and understanding of the facts behind both the virus and the vaccines. This enlightenment will empower me to make educated decisions rather than fear-based ones.

How can you begin to move towards fulfillment at this level of needs? In other words, what actions do you believe are necessary?

Coronavirus: With the many unknown characteristics of the Coronavirus, I could begin educating myself through the proper channels using peer-reviewed sources by experts in the field rather than turning to the media and political opinions. I can change my daily habits of listening to the news and instead become educated through science.

Vaccines: With the desire to become knowledgeable regarding the vaccine, I can actively choose to educate myself by reviewing factual data coming out of the vaccine trials, watching FDA panel reviews, and engaging in podcasts from experienced doctors and healthcare professionals.

Why is it vital for you to elevate and fulfill these needs? (Reflect upon your purpose and burning desires to help answer this question)

The result of elevating my physical safety needs will enhance my overall safety needs. As this level of growth becomes strengthened, I can begin to work on the next level: psychological needs.

As my fears are eliminated, I will become the courageous example my children need. If I truly want my kids to live a life full of faith and abundance, I need to step up and show them how to attain these components, especially in moments of adversity. If I remain in a state of fear, they will be influenced to do the same.

Where might you experience obstacles or roadblocks to fulfilling these needs? (Use Chapter 9 on *Overcoming Obstacles* to help answer this question)

Since the possible solutions to my fears of COVID 19 and the virus are rooted in consciously educating myself by turning to factual-based sources and peer-reviewed articles, the roadblocks for both solutions are similar. The one obstacle I have experienced in my past is psychological dependence while having a fixed mindset. I relied on non-factual sources for data throughout the early phases of the pandemic, contributing to the hindrances on my hierarchy of needs. For a time, my thoughts were considerably fixed, and I was not open to looking at other sources of information outside of the news and social circles. If I genuinely want to become knowledgeable about both the virus and the vaccine, I need to let go of this reliance on others and become open to using my own brain.

Who might you need support from to make these changes?

> To move into a state of awareness and knowledge, I will require time to educate myself properly. To help with this, I will need the support of my husband.

> Additionally, I will require guidance and knowledge from experts in the appropriate fields of science. I will lean on those who have an honest and unbiased opinion and rely on facts.

Actions: With a burning desire to feel safe again, working towards living a fulfilled life, I began to apply my learnings to formulate critical steps necessary for growth.

> **Specific:** What are your goals for fulfilling your physical safety needs?

> My goal to elevate my physical safety needs involves properly educating myself about both the vaccine and the virus using factual and unbiased data from various experts.

> **Measurable:** How will you track or measure your progress with these goals?

> I will commit to thirty minutes a day of education to further understand the virus and vaccine, moving into a state of awareness. I will track this action in my daily goal tracker.

Attainable: Are these goals achievable for you, and do you have the power to activate them? Explain.

Yes, these goals are attainable, and I can control whether they get fulfilled. The one component I do not control is the time it will take to become educated. This uncertainty is because both the virus and the vaccine are concurrently being studied by experts and will require time for scientific evaluations to establish factual conclusions.

Relevant: Do these goals move you closer to reaching your mission and greater vision? How?

Yes, these goals will move me closer to achieving my burning desire to grow through the toxicity and fears that took over my life. I will become realigned to my values through this overcoming, bringing peace and prosperity into my home.

Time Frame: When do you want to achieve each goal?

I will implement these goals immediately, working in unison with fulfilling the first level of needs: my basic needs. By committing to thirty minutes of research to understand the virus and vaccine over one month, I will gain a significant amount of knowledge regarding the actual risks associated with both. After one month, I will reassess this goal, ensuring I continue to support my education and awareness of the vaccinations and the COVID-19 virus.

Economic Safety Needs

Acknowledge: An individual's economic safety becomes threatened when their jobs, finances, or personal freedoms are at risk. As the globe entered a pandemic status, businesses closed, leaving many without jobs, which hindered their finances. The governments of many countries stepped in to provide aid at varying capacities; however, this took time to establish. For some, the damage was done before this support came. Although my family never experienced a loss of income through COVID-19, I experienced a significant amount of anxiety over it. Additionally, as restrictions and vaccine mandates rolled out, both Kelsey and I experienced a significant impact on our personal freedoms. We were no longer able to live our lives freely as we once were. As you can see, my economic safety needs were impacted on a psychological and physical level.

Assessment: Knowing the extreme pressures and anxieties I experienced with our overall economic security, it was necessary to complete an in-depth review to understand these impacts fully.

> **What** contributes to a lack of fulfillment of your job, finances, and personal freedoms? Are these causes because of outside factors or your own habits and actions?

>> *Job & Financial Security:* As mandates for vaccines began to roll out, some businesses imposed vaccine requirements. The outcome of making our decisions around inoculations in alignment with our values led to my overwhelming fear of my husband losing his job, our source of income. I endured many moments of tears and breakdowns, feeling pressured by outside forces to do something that did not align with my

values. I became stuck in the "what if" game, playing out all the possible outcomes that could go wrong.

Personal Security: As the government rolled out restrictions and mandates, I became consumed with the possibility of losing our personal freedoms to live life through our values. I became frustrated with the handcuffs placed upon the citizens of our nations. I knew in my heart that things were not right as the leaders of our countries pinned vaccinated against unvaccinated. Individuals were verbally assaulted because they had different values and made other choices. It became clear that our personal freedoms to live our life normally and freely were conditional on the government's guidelines. You could not live freely in Canada unless you accepted the vaccine and used the vaccine passport. The government of Canada imposed such strict measures for travel that many felt as though they were trapped, our family included. I truly experienced a hindrance to my personal security, and I no longer felt safe living in the country I was born in.

When did you first notice hindrances to these needs?

Job & Financial Security: Although our family never endured actual hindrances to our job or financial security, the fears we experienced felt as real as if we did. My worries began as individuals lost their jobs and became magnified as businesses and governments rolled out vaccine mandates in Canada.

Personal Security: I noticed hindrances to my personal security when the government limited my freedom of choice by imposing mandates, including vaccine requirements.

What does the ultimate fulfillment of these needs look like for you? What does your ideal economic safety look like for your job, finances, and personal security?

> *Job & Financial Security:* Ultimate fulfillment of these needs would involve knowing that both job and financial security are a reality.

> *Personal Security:* My ideal outcome to fulfill these needs would be having the complete assurance that my personal rights and freedom of choice were protected without condemnation.

How can you begin to move towards fulfillment at this level of needs? In other words, what actions do you believe are necessary?

> *Job & Financial Security:* Fear of my husband losing his job and our source of income was simply that, just a fear. Knowing this brings clarity to the necessary action needed to elevate these needs: psychological rewiring of my fearful thoughts to those that are empowering. To support this, having intimate conversations with Kelsey around the worst-case scenario and creating a game plan for those unplanned moments would help. We could brainstorm alternative income streams, review our budget weekly, and develop a financial strategy. To enhance this process of rewiring my thoughts, I could apply the four-step process to elevating my thoughts through

autosuggestion and partake in healthy daily inputs such as reading books and listening to podcasts.

Personal Security: To fulfill my personal security needs, the first thing I could do is begin to understand the charter of rights and freedom in more detail. This knowledge would help me distinguish between the fears that have festered and the actual strain on my individual rights. Additionally, Kelsey and I could begin to have conversations about alternate countries to reside in that have protected and upheld the rights and freedoms of their citizens.

Why is it essential for you to elevate and fulfill these needs? (Reflect upon your purpose and burning desires to help answer this question)

Job & Financial Security: It is crucial to feeling a sense of financial security to plug the energy leaks that would otherwise occur in a state of fear. By reducing the energy lost, I can shift my focus and time towards the areas of my life that need attention. By moving from fear to faith, I can tap into these higher vibrational thoughts to bring energy to other areas of my life, such as my faith, relationships, health, and calling.

Personal Security: Everyone needs to have freedom of choice with their rights protected under the law as this allows one to live entirely through their key pillars. To truly reach self-actualization in my life, I know that I must meet this level of needs. Additionally, if I want my children to have the opportunity to attain self-actualization, they must also have this need fulfilled.

An impact on one's personal security is an impact on future generations.

Where might you experience obstacles or roadblocks to fulfilling these needs? (Use Chapter 9 on *Overcoming Obstacles* to help answer this question)

Job & Financial Security: Potential obstacles to elevating my thoughts and emotions around job and financial security is procrastinating the work necessary to make these changes. Because the alterations required are at a psychological level rather than a physical level, these changes can be regarded as an unimportant task.

Personal Security: To gratify my personal security needs and those of my kids and future generations, I may need to consider the life-altering choice of relocating. An obstacle to making this decision would be the fear of failure. Thoughts of "what if I don't like this change or it doesn't work for our family" are prominent.

Who might you need support from to make these changes?

Job & Financial Security: To help with these changes necessary, I will need the support and engagement in conversations with my husband.

Personal Security: To enhance my knowledge of personal rights and freedoms, consulting a professional such as a lawyer would be ideal. Seeking this expertise will ensure I get factual information from a reputable source.

Actions: If I truly wanted to experience peace and abundance within my economic safety needs, I needed to be open to receiving new truths and making changes towards prosperity. Using the discoveries throughout my assessment, I created specific, measurable, actionable, relevant, and time-specific goals to help raise my fulfillment at this level.

Specific: What are your goals for fulfilling your job, financial and personal security needs?

Job & Financial Security: My goal is to shift my lower frequency thoughts and emotions laden with fear to those of a positive and uplifting nature by applying the four-step process to elevating all toxic thoughts. This process includes: developing awareness of my thoughts, having a desire and willingness to change these thoughts, creating a new empowering thought, and downloading this new thought into my neural network through autosuggestion. I will prioritize fifteen minutes a day to apply this process. Additionally, I will also read a personal growth book for fifteen minutes and listen to a podcast every day to further support this transformation.

Personal Security: To begin sifting between my fears and actual personal security hindrances, I will prioritize fifteen minutes a day to review reputable information regarding the rights and freedoms protected under the law. At times this may involve seeking guidance from professionals.

Measurable: How will you track or measure your progress with these goals?

> *Job & Financial Security:* I will add fifteen minutes of applying the four-step process to my thoughts, reading for fifteen minutes a day and listening to one podcast daily to my tracking tool.

> *Personal Security:* Again, I will add the goal of prioritizing fifteen minutes a day towards educating myself about the protected rights and freedoms to my tracker.

Attainable: Are these goals achievable for you, and do you have the power to activate them? Explain.

> Yes, I have the power to activate and fulfill both goals since they are constructed and reliant on my own actions versus relying on others.

Relevant: Do these goals move you closer to reaching your greater vision? How?

> A result of elevating my economic safety will enhance my overall safety needs. As I solidify this fundamental level within my hierarchy of growth, I will be able to begin the process of satisfying the next level: psychological needs.

Time Frame: When do you want to achieve each goal?

Job & Financial Security: Since it takes three months to implement a new habit, I will diligently rewire my habitual thought processes over this required time frame. I will accomplish this by applying the four-step process to elevating my thoughts, reading an educational book for fifteen minutes a day, and listening to a podcast daily over a three-month time frame. After this period, I will obtain a new and positive thought process, reducing my job and financial security fears.

Personal Security: I will prioritize fifteen minutes a day to educate myself about an individual's protected rights and freedoms for one month. After this time frame, I will have elevated my knowledge, and I will also re-evaluate if I need to set a new goal to continue my education.

Psychological Needs: Social & Esteem Needs

As I went to work on growing my basic physical and safety needs, I found myself slowly being released from the grips of these lower levels. I became more open and available for growth at the next stage, my psychological needs. This stage comprises two necessities that include social and esteem needs. Here, I experienced the most negative impact on my overall hierarchy of growth, hindering my ability to move towards self-fulfillment.

Social Needs

Acknowledge: Since an individual's social needs involve reaching a sense of belonging and acceptance, something I lacked throughout

COVID-19, I realized I was starving for connection. I not only felt like an outcast amid my fears, but I also experienced rejection through my environment as our nations expressed shame and contempt towards one another.

Assessment: Through acknowledging the hindrance to my social needs, I learned that I was experiencing both a disconnect from others internally and externally. Using a series of questions geared towards deepening my self-evaluations, I will be able to uncover the contributors to the separation I felt.

> **What** is contributing to a lack of fulfillment of your social needs? Are the contributors an external cause from your environment, or are they because of your thought processes?
>
> > *Thought Processes:* The psychological impact I experienced during the early stage of COVID-19 was intense as my thoughts and emotions were stuck in a toxic loop. They had created a lasting pattern within my brain, leading me to feel and think of separation and division in all areas of my life. I realized that the cause for these thoughts and feelings was because of my weakened faith pillar, experiencing severe disconnection to that which is greater. Additionally, the toxic and lower energy inputs from my environments and associations only added to the division I felt.
> >
> > *Outer Environment:* Numerous events contributed to physical separation and division from those in my life. These outcomes that severely impacted my social needs were the significant contributors to my dark days through COVID-19. They included: stay-at-home orders, business closures, halting extracurricular

activity, isolation periods, mask mandates, vaccination mandates, contempt expressed by leaders of our nations, and individuals fearing socialization.

When did you first notice hindrances to these needs?

I first noticed the hindrance to my social needs when stay-at-home orders were released. This internal sense of loneliness and disconnection deepened as I became isolated with a newborn baby at home. My support network made up of family and friends just disappeared.

What does the ultimate fulfillment of these needs look like for you?

Thought Processes: To reach gratification within my inner world, I would be experiencing thoughts of connection, unity, and belonging.

Outer Environment: Components that would contribute to the ultimate fulfillment of my sense of connection to the outer world includes:

- Ability to socialize with family and friends freely without restrictions and mandates.
- Being able to connect without judgment, criticism, or anger expressed by family, friends, and acquaintances due to the different values and choices made during this time.
- Experiencing a sense of love and belonging within my community, regardless of your race, background, values, and decisions made.

> A community of acceptance for who I am is
> crucial to fulfilling my social needs.

How can you begin to move towards fulfillment
at this level of needs? In other words, what actions
do you believe are necessary?

> *Thought Processes:* To experience the thoughts and
> emotions of connection to Source or God, I could
> begin to read spiritual books and listen to podcasts.
> Furthermore, to support the elevation of my social
> needs, I need to apply the four-step process to alter
> my thoughts of separation to those of unity and
> connection. As you will learn in the coming pages,
> the process of elevating my thoughts had a profound
> impact on all types of lower energy psychological
> complexes. Every kind of negative thought requires
> a unique positive thought to replace it. Although the
> specifics of each thought were different, the process
> of rewiring them was the same for each.

> *Outer Environment:* Ways to connect with family
> and friends included breaking the isolation
> mandates, being creative to find activities that we
> could do outside, and using video conference calls
> to communicate with others. A potential solution to
> making new connections is to continue participating
> in permitted activities. Through this, I would have
> the opportunity to connect with others outside of my
> current social circle.

Why is it vital for you to elevate and fulfill these
needs? (Reflect upon your purpose and burning
desires to help answer this question)

Through elevating my connection to Source or God, I will begin to repair my broken faith pillars. Moreover, as I meet my social needs where I experience a sense of love and belonging, the relationships in my life will also strengthen and flourish. A by-product of this will lead to the enhancement of my other pillars.

Where might you experience obstacles or roadblocks to fulfilling these needs? (Use Chapter 9 on *Overcoming Obstacles* to help answer this question)

Thought Processes: The effort required to elevate my thoughts are on the unseen psychological level; therefore, I can easily disregard the significance of this work. A potential obstacle to elevating these thoughts would be procrastination.

Outer Environment: An individual's sense of connectedness to the outside world can be severely impacted by influences outside their control. Because of this, potential obstacles to elevating my social needs would include the fact that I cannot manage what goes on in my outer environment. However, I can control my choice to partake in specific settings.

Who might you need support from to make these changes?

Thought Processes: Transforming one's thoughts requires time and commitment. Again, my husband would be someone I would lean on for support during this process.

Outer Environment: To succeed at elevating my sense of connection with those around me, I would need the support of family and friends.

Actions: The intense need for connection within my psychological and external environments was the fuel that drove my desire for change. Relying on my assessments, I generated meaningful goals to move toward my higher self.

Specific: What are your goals for fulfilling your social needs? These goals can be either internal focused, external focused, or both.

Thought Processes: My goal is to shift my thoughts of separation and isolation to those of unity and connectedness to God and others around me. I will accomplish this by applying the four-step process fifteen minutes a day to alter my thoughts. Additionally, I will enhance my inputs from my environment, including reading a book for fifteen minutes and listening to a personal growth podcast every day.

Outer Environment: To elevate my connectedness to those around me, I will look for ways to socialize with one individual per week within my family and friends.

Measurable: How will you track or measure your progress with these goals?

Thought Processes: To monitor progress towards this goal, I will ensure I added fifteen minutes of applying the four-step process, fifteen minutes of reading and listening to a podcast to my daily tracking tool. You will notice this goal overlaps with others. This redundancy is significant because it concludes that I have found a single solution to multiple problems. As a result, my goals will become streamlined, making it easier to achieve them.

Outer Environment: It may be more challenging to track this goal since outside factors highly influence it; however, I can control my actions and attitude towards connecting with family and friends. A measurable goal is to reach out and connect with at least one individual per week.

Attainable: Are these goals obtainable for you, and do you have the power to activate them? Explain.

Yes, these goals are attainable as long as I have the ability to activate them. I cannot control what other individuals decide, but I can control my efforts and actions.

Relevant: Do these goals move you closer to reaching your greater vision? How?

Through meeting my desires to feel a sense of belonging and connectedness to God and others around me, my relationships will prosper. As my social needs become satisfied, I will be moving toward my burning desire to experience unity within my faith, family, and community.

Time Frame: When do you want to implement each goal?

Thought Processes: As you have learned in the prior section, economic needs, I will diligently apply the four-step process fifteen minutes a day to alter my thoughts over a three-month time frame to achieve success in rewiring my cognitive processes to be those of a positive nature. Again, this will be supported by reading fifteen minutes a day of a personal growth book and listening to an enlightening podcast daily.

Outer Environment: I will begin to reach out to family and friends and prioritize connecting with one individual weekly for three months to elevate my social needs.

Esteem Needs

As you have learned earlier, an individual's esteem needs are primarily composed of their psychological processing where our beliefs are stored. Since our thoughts and emotions formulate our beliefs, I will share an in-depth personal review of my esteem needs using the four significant impacts on an individual's thoughts as a framework. These impacts include Inner Dialogue, Stimulus & Energy Levels, Self-Esteem & Egotism, Ignorance & Knowledge. In Chapter 2, I openly shared the mental battles my husband and I went through between anxiety and depression, resulting from these four significant influences. Because COVID-19 impacted my psychological needs the most, my evaluations and actions will be significantly more in-depth than the basic needs.

Acknowledge: With the onset of the Coronavirus, it became a fertile ground for negative thinking processes to bloom in the minds of many, including myself. I recognized this cognitive shift in my thought processes at many different pandemic stages. My thinking processes began to transform, focusing on what I didn't want to happen versus putting my mind on the things I did want. This cognitive shift became a significant contributor to the anxieties I experienced.

Assessment: With a burning desire to reach a state of peace and contentment, I needed to take an in-depth approach to assess my esteem needs. To accomplish this, I used the 6W framework in combination with the four major influences on an individual's psychological processes.

> **What** is contributing to a lack of fulfillment of your esteem needs?

> > ***Inner Dialogue:*** I became overwhelmed by the negative narratives spoken throughout the pandemic and allowed the lower energy thoughts to overtake my mind. As things unfolded and more data rolled out, my narratives shifted through the different stages that ensued. To help you understand these transitions in the lower energy realm, I have broken these thoughts into different phases of the pandemic. You will notice some concerns remaining present throughout.

> > *Early Stage of COVID-19*

> > - What if I or someone I love got sick or, worse, died from COVID?
> > - What if my husband lost his job due to COVID?

- What if we don't see family again due to COVID?
- What if this pandemic lasts forever?
- What if I lose control of my physical and mental health?
- How long will my husband's anxiety and depression last?
- How long will my anxieties last?
- How do I raise my kids in this world, and what if my kids become consumed with fear?

Vaccine Roll-Out Stage

- Why would the FDA and government roll out an experimental vaccine?
- Why hasn't there been a significant amount of follow-up on the safety of the vaccines?
- What if the government mandates the experimental vaccine?
- What if I or someone I love dies from the vaccine?
- What if my husband lost his job due to being unvaccinated?
- What if this pandemic goes on for years?
- How do I raise my kids in this world, and what if my kids become consumed with fear?
- What if the government continues to censor our doctors and scientists?
- Why is there a lack of transparency by the large public health organizations?
- What if the government continues to overstep, taking away our personal freedoms?

Stimulus & Energy Levels: As the world began to shut down, the positive and enlightening energies that were once present began to disappear as the negative and lower energy thoughts of fear, scarcity, judgment, criticism, and anger took over. This toxicity drained my mind, body, and environment, all three of my energy zones. Using these three zones to guide my assessments, I will break down how I determined my energy leaks, ultimately impacting my esteem needs.

Cognitive Energy Zone: The cognitive energy zone is influenced by our intimate thought processes, also known as our self-speech. As you have learned earlier, my inner world was plagued with negative thoughts and emotions, severely depleting my cognitive energy zone. Resultantly, I had entered a state of anxiety.

Physical Energy Zone: As businesses closed and stress entered my life, my physical energy-filling routines were thrown off course, leaving me feeling empty and drained. Significant contributors to this depletion included: the closure of fitness facilities, stopping self-care regimes as wellness businesses closed, and the lack of sleep.

Environmental Energy Zone: Soon after the COVID-19 outbreak, my environmental energy zone shifted from positive to negative. Substantive contributors to this included: our once positive social circle becoming toxic as their mindsets transitioned from positive to negative and the constant bombardment of alerts or advertisements regarding the fear, anger, and adverse outcomes caused by COVID-19.

Self-Esteem & Egotism: The fearful expressions of ego that took root in our nations included comparison, judgment, criticism, and anger. These emotions not only infested the globe but also took hold of my mind and heart as fears became embedded in my home. It was only a matter of time before hazardous levels of egotism crept their way back into my life as my mind became encapsulated by fear. To help streamline this process of assessing my thoughts of self-importance, I have utilized the six unhealthy expressions of ego as my guideposts.

Accumulation and Ownership of Things: Along with the fear of Kelsey losing his job, I feared that we would have to give up our house and all of our possessions. We had a five-year plan to build our dream home debt-free; was this plan going to be derailed? The thought of losing the attainment of our goals and dreams created the springboard into scarcity mode. Who would we be if we lost our source of income, home, and possessions?

Achievements and Weaknesses: The belief of "I am what I do" is a common thought by those who have allowed their successes and achievements to define their self-worth. These thoughts flourish when one feels their accomplishments could be slipping away, myself included.

- I feared the potential outcome of Kelsey losing his job and all his achievements in his career.
- Additionally, I became consumed with the anxieties of raising my kids in a world of fear as their social and interactive skills were significantly hindered. I began comparing

my kids' behaviors to others and tying any development concerns to my abilities as a mom. Feeling inadequate on numerous occasions, I began to tie my self-worth to my parenting throughout this season.

Personality & Reputation: It was embedded into our brains the "right" way to behave through this pandemic by the media, government, workplaces, and specialists in the healthcare and scientific communities. If you didn't follow what was communicated, you were judged and criticized, especially by leaders in positions of power. This environment became fertile for the egoic traits of approval seeking to take root. Thoughts of this nature included:

- What would people think of how I approached the restrictions and mandates?
- What will individuals say as I take my kids out into public like a grocery store or a park?
- What would people say if I did get the vaccine? What would people think if I didn't?

Physical Attributes: While fitness facilities and health and wellness businesses closed their doors, I recognized that I was worried about losing my physical health. There were small moments when I found myself comparing my current physique to my past physical achievements—criticizing my physical strength, size of muscles, and the amount of fat I had on my body.

Separation: I recognized that my coping mechanism to deal with our nation's significant scrutiny and criticism was judging or criticizing back. These actions led to me believing that I was separate from everyone and, at times, that I was better than others. As I share the egoic thoughts present in my life, please know that my heart does not want to hurt anyone. My goal here is to help you understand what these unhealthy expressions of egotism look like. I hope my openness can help you open up about your own judgments, recognize them, and accept ownership of them, no matter how bad they are.

Early COVID-19 Judgements:

- This person got too close to me; they are disrespectful.
- That person is not wearing a mask; how inconsiderate.
- That person is touching all the produce; that's disgusting and rude.
- Those who don't sanitize are selfish and do not take the proper precautions.

Later COVID Judgements:

- Why are the low-risk people so scared? They have not educated themselves on the virus.
- People who wear masks outside or in their vehicles are full of fear.
- Who would get a vaccine developed in under a year? These people were not thinking for themselves.
- Those who supported the vaccine mandates and passports are OK to have their personal

freedoms taken away; their own fears control them.

Independence from God: As you know, I was embarking on my spiritual and faith journey leading up to the pandemic. This already fragile faith pillar crumbled when COVID-19 happened. When I hit my low during the pandemic, I realized I lost my faith in being connected to everyone and everything, including Source.

Ignorance & Knowledge: Naturally, as one encounters new events and experiences, they will have some ignorance, including myself.

Early Stage of COVID-19: I understood that I did not know the facts regarding the Coronavirus. Because of this ignorance, I developed a dependency on news outlets, large public health organizations, and governments to provide data. At the time, frozen with fear, I found it challenging to use my own brain and resources to complete my own factual and evidence-based research.

Later Stage of COVID-19: As time passed, an incredible amount of conflicting information regarding the virus and the vaccine surfaced. Healthcare professionals, scientists, doctors, governments, and health care organizations had opposing views on the risks associated with the virus and the immunizations. This incongruency contributed to severe distrust in the government and public health organizations. There was a shift where leaders, influencers, and media began to express opinions rather than facts, leading to feelings of frustration and confusion.

When did you first notice hindrances to these needs?

The impacts on my psychological health, precisely my esteem needs, began within the first few months of the Coronavirus outbreak. As time progressed, my inner dialogue, energy levels, egotism, and ignorance fueled my lower vibrational thoughts and emotions, turning them into mental health concerns of anxiety.

What does the ultimate fulfillment of these needs look like for you?

Inner Dialogue: Having an inner dialogue free from the judgments and criticisms and rooted in an empowering nature will significantly elevate my esteem needs.

Stimulus & Energy Levels: Fulfilling my energy levels will require identifying and plugging the energy leaks while finding ways to elevate my cognitive, physical and environmental energy zones.

Self-Esteem & Egotism: True gratification of my self-esteem will require eradicating the lower energy thoughts connected to the six primary expressions of ego: accumulation and ownership of things, achievements and weaknesses, personality and reputation, physical attributes, separation, and independence from God.

Ignorance & Knowledge: Having an open and growth-oriented mind is crucial to elevating my esteem needs. Additionally, it is consequential to break free from dependency on others for information and to step into taking responsibility for gathering my factual information.

How can you begin to move towards fulfillment at this level of needs? In other words, what actions do you believe are necessary?

Inner Dialogue: By applying a four-step process to elevating all toxic thoughts, my esteem needs will begin to prosper.

Stimulus & Energy Levels: Since all three energy zones impact my overall energy levels, I need to identify the actions necessary to enhance each of these individual zones.

Cognitive Energy Zone: By elevating my inner dialogue, the result of this action will enhance my cognitive energy zone.

Physical Energy Zone: Actions necessary to plug my physical energy leaks include establishing a workout regime without relying on fitness centers, finding ways to partake in regular self-care activities, and prioritizing sleep.

Environmental Energy Zone: To improve the energy within my environmental zone, I can: set boundaries with negative individuals, reduce participation in settings that are considered an energy leak, and eliminate all lower energy inputs in my home environment.

Self-Esteem & Egotism: The process of moving towards my higher self, letting go of my false identifications, is identical to that of the four-step process of elevating one's inner dialogue. To reiterate this process in the context of ego: I will need to become aware of the egoic thoughts present, have a willingness to change my misidentifications, create a new empowering thought free from the six expressions of ego, and rewire my cognitive processes using autosuggestion.

Ignorance & Knowledge: To begin elevating my knowledge, I need to break free from the dependency on others to provide factual information about the virus and vaccine. I had a very independent and open mindset leading up to the pandemic. A shift from a fixed mentality to an open one is necessary to reach this place again. With my background as a Chemical Engineer, I am trained to follow the science through reputable research; therefore, it's time to foster and apply this skill set. Earlier I mentioned the actions of completing reputable research around the virus and vaccine to enhance my safety needs. These goals are applicable here as well since they will elevate my knowledge.

Why is it essential for you to elevate and fulfill these needs? (Reflect upon your purpose and burning desires to help answer this question)

Through refining my thoughts and emotions to move from fear to faith, all my key pillars will begin to strengthen. Instilling positive thoughts will enhance my faith as I eliminate my worries. My mental and physical health will improve as I reduce anxiety spurred by my cognitive processes. My relationships will flourish as I approach them with positivity. My calling as a coach will prosper as I become more equipped to help others move through their own trying times.

Where might you experience obstacles or roadblocks to fulfilling these needs? (Use Chapter 9 on *Overcoming Obstacles* to help answer this question)

Inner Dialogue: The transformation journey of an individual's inner dialogue is invisible to the outer world. They may see new outcomes that you experience, but they are not aware of the conscious decision you have made to elevate your thoughts. As I have mentioned earlier, a potential obstacle to changes on the psychological level includes procrastination, as it can be a challenge to prioritize the unseen transformations.

Stimulus & Energy Levels: Potential roadblocks to elevating my overall energy levels are dependent on the specific energy zone.

Cognitive Energy Zone: The potential roadblock to enhancing my cognitive energy zone is identical to what I shared for elevating inner dialogue.

Physical Energy Zone: To elevate my physical energy zone, the obstacle that comes to mind is approval seeking. Since this work requires prioritizing myself and focusing on self-care, I may wonder if I'm being selfish by prioritizing self-care when others need me.

Environmental Energy Zone: As I look to improve my environmental energy zone, I will be required to set boundaries with outside influences, including friends and family. A potential obstacle to this is approval-seeking.

Self-Esteem & Egotism: The journey of eradicating ego and moving towards my higher self requires psychological and behavioral changes. Since our thoughts and emotions determine our actions and behavior, I will manifest the desired behavior change if I focus primarily on altering my thoughts. Knowing this, the potential roadblocks I may experience are procrastination on the psychological level and approval seeking on the behavior level.

Ignorance & Knowledge: As you have learned already, a significant hindrance I experienced regarding knowledge throughout COVID-19 was the dependency on others for information.

Who might you need support from to make these changes?

Necessary support to help with elevating my esteem needs would be that of my husband. We are a team recognizing that we have a profound impact on the success of each other's goals.

Action: As a result of the comprehensive assessment completed around my esteem needs and the profound impact on my psychological processes, I was well equipped to identify the SMART goals necessary for growth.

Specific: What are your goals for fulfilling your esteem needs? If applicable, consider setting one for each of the four primary influences on an individual's esteem needs.

Inner Dialogue: The process of elevating my inner dialogue goes hand in hand with the other psychological goals I have set throughout my hierarchy of needs. My goal of elevating my inner dialogue will be to commit to reading fifteen minutes a day from an educational book and listening to a podcast daily. To further enhance my goals of elevating my inner dialogue, I will also spend fifteen minutes a day consciously applying the four-step process of reprograming my mind.

Stimulus & Energy Levels: The specific goals I have set to improve my overall energy levels are specific to each energy zone.

Cognitive Energy Zone: Goals to elevate my cognitive energy zone are the same as those I have shared for improving my Inner Dialogue.

Physical Energy Zone: As mentioned under my physiological needs, a goal I have identified is to work out five days a week for 45 minutes, including weight training, kickboxing, pilates, running, and yoga.

Environmental Energy Zone: To elevate my environmental energy levels, my goal will be to establish healthy boundaries saying no to the environments that are considered an energy leak in my life. These boundaries involve eliminating the triggers of my negative thoughts and emotions, such as the news, negative TV shows, toxic videos, advertisements, and specific individuals.

Self-Esteem & Egotism: With the desire to reduce and eliminate the ego that flourished during COVID-19, my goal is identical to what I have shared with you for elevating my inner dialogue. I will apply the same four-step process to raising the frequency of my thoughts to be in alignment with my higher self, free from ego.

Ignorance & Knowledge: To enhance my knowledge through COVID-19, my goals here are the same goals I have shared to improve my safety needs. These include prioritizing thirty minutes a day of educating myself about both the vaccine and the virus and fifteen minutes a day to review reputable information regarding the rights and freedoms protected under the law.

Measurable: How will you track or measure your progress with these goals?

Inner Dialogue: I will time block my calendar to ensure I prioritize reading fifteen minutes a day, listening to educational audio each day, and spending 15 minutes applying the four-step process to rewiring my thinking processes. I will monitor these goals in my daily tracking tool.

Stimulus & Energy Levels: I will add both goals, working out and setting healthy boundaries, to my daily tracker. To ensure the success of my exercise goals, I will set firm appointments in my calendar, prioritizing the times I will be working out during the week.

Self-Esteem & Egotism: Since the process of eliminating my egotistical thoughts are identical to elevating inner dialogue, my daily tracker will monitor these goals as one.

Ignorance & Knowledge: As mentioned earlier, I will add two goals of enhancing my knowledge to my daily tracker. These two goals are completing thirty minutes a day of educating myself about both the vaccine and the virus and fifteen minutes a day to understand my rights and freedoms protected under the law.

Attainable: Are these goals achievable for you, and do you have the power to activate them? Explain.

Yes, these goals for each: Inner Dialogue, Stimulus & Energy Levels, Self-Esteem & Egotism, Ignorance & Knowledge are attainable and rely on my commitment to follow through and prioritize them in my schedule.

Relevant: Do these goals move you closer to reaching your greater vision? How?

> Through growing in all four areas that influence my esteem needs, I will begin to heal my psychological health concern of anxiety. As a result, this will strengthen my health in combination with all the other pillars of my life. As my esteem needs become satisfied, space will begin to open for creativity, growth, and self-fulfillment. This foundation will propel me into the next level of development, self-actualization.

Time Frame: When do you want to implement each goal?

> *Inner Dialogue:* After three months of consistent application of the four-step process, reading a book for fifteen minutes a day, and listening to a personal development podcast daily, I will enhance my inner dialogue and self-speech.

> *Stimulus & Energy Levels:* The timeline to complete each goal is specific to each energy zone.

>> *Cognitive Energy Zone:* See timeline for Inner Dialogue goals.

>> *Physical Energy Zone:* I will enhance my physical energy levels within three months of committing to a healthy exercise regime encompassing 45-minute workouts five days a week.

>> *Environmental Energy Zone:* By eliminating the energy leaks due to my environment over three

months, my surroundings will become those that will enhance my energy levels instead of draining them.

Self-Esteem & Egotism: Since the process of altering one's egoic thoughts is identical to elevating one's inner dialogue, the time frame required to eliminate the presence of ego is also the same. After three months of consistent application of the four-step process, reading a book for fifteen minutes a day, and listening to a personal development podcast daily, I will reduce and eliminate the ego in my life.

Ignorance & Knowledge: After one month of prioritizing thirty minutes a day to become educated about both the vaccine and the virus and fifteen minutes a day to understand the rights and freedoms, I will enhance my knowledge contributing to the elevation of my esteem needs.

Self-Actualization Needs

Acknowledge: With both my basic and psychological needs being threatened, achieving fulfillment during this time became very challenging for both myself and my family. If we do not achieve some stability in these lower needs, the foundation can crumble at any moment, erasing all progress towards self-fulfillment. This outcome is what transpired for me during COVID-19.

Assessment: Naturally, as my basic and psychological needs suffered, so did my self-actualization needs. To summarize what you have learned already, here are the significant impacts that led to me living an unfulfilled life lacking purpose.

What is contributing to a lack of fulfillment of
your self-actualization needs?

- I lost sight of my greater purpose as my vision
  blurred by the stress and anxieties I experienced.
- My faith and health pillars collapsed during
  COVID-19, which led to strains on the other
  values in my life.
- During the early phase of the pandemic, my daily
  decisions were based on emotions of fear rather
  than factual knowledge.
- My inner dialogue and cognitive processes shifted
  from higher frequency thoughts to those of a lower
  frequency.
- The bombardment of negative stimuli and draining
  of my overall energy levels contributed to my poor
  psychological processes.
- I had allowed the many expressions of ego into
  my life, which began to dominate my thoughts,
  actions, and outcomes.
- My mind was focused on preservation and survival,
  deterring thriving and prosperous thoughts.

When did you first notice hindrances to these needs?

I was pulled from the higher levels of needs, including
self-fulfillment, when the pandemic began. As my
basic and psychological needs suffered, cracks and
holes formed in the foundation required to reach the
state of self-actualization.

What does the ultimate fulfillment of these needs
look like for you?

The complete fulfillment of my self-actualization needs is reaching a state where I am purposefully living my life through my values while achieving self-fulfillment through helping others.

How can you begin to move towards fulfillment at this level of needs? In other words, what actions do you believe are necessary?

A requirement to meet my self-actualization needs is to fulfill my lower-level basic and psychological needs. The required actions include the ones I have shared for each level of growth, including my physiological, safety, social, and esteem needs.

Why is it vital for you to elevate and fulfill these needs? (Reflect upon your purpose and burning desires to help answer this question)

It is crucial for me to reach this level of needs as I will be fulfilling my mission statement, which includes my ultimate purpose, vision, and burning desire. To reinforce the significance of reaching this level of growth, I will share this declaration again here:

My ultimate purpose is to live a life full of growth and abundance in my faith, relationships, finances, mental & physical health, and calling. My vision is to create a positive impact everywhere I go, leaving a shining light in one soul to the next. My burning desire is to grow through the toxicity and fears that take over my life at any given point in time, always realigning to my values, and bringing peace into our home.

I desire unity within my family and community and realignment with my higher self, God.

Where might you experience obstacles or roadblocks to fulfilling these needs? (Use Chapter 9 on *Overcoming Obstacles* to help answer this question)

Potential obstacles to fulfilling self-actualization include failing to meet the goals set at the lower-level needs. Refer to each level, considering the goals identified and their potential roadblocks to understanding what may hinder my progression towards self-fulfillment.

Who might you need support from to make these changes?

Individuals that I will require support from as I elevate through the varying levels of needs include all of those that I have acknowledged throughout my assessment.

Actions: Naturally, as I meet my basic and psychological needs, the outcome will lead to a shift from discontent to self-fulfillment. My burning desire for change may have started the process of elevation, but it will be my dedication to growth in all areas that will lead to ultimate gratification and the manifestation of my higher self. It is important to emphasize that every desired transformation that I identified within my basic and psychological needs are the same changes I would enlist to live in alignment with my highest calling, reaching self-actualization. Every mindset shift and persistent daily habit takes one step closer to self-fulfillment. I encourage you to go back and reread this chapter to understand that every action of growth identified will lay the foundation for reaching self-actualization.

Summary

Because of my intense burning desire to live my life with purpose and make this world a better place, I established an unwavering commitment to each of the goals I set. I completely transformed my life by elevating each level within my hierarchy of needs. Eventually, I learned to let go of all the dominating fears, restored faith in my ability to create any life I desired, and established a trust in God. Experiencing the journey of God-realization is hard to explain because it does not rely on any of the five senses. It is this feeling deep inside, a knowing that everything will be OK. As you walk towards self-fulfillment and reach this state full of purpose, love, and abundance, you will notice others may grow alongside you as the light shining brightly on your path can shed light onto others.

"Recognize that every interaction you have is an opportunity to make a positive impact on others." ~ Shep Hyken

CHAPTER 11

The Outcome of Activating My Plan for Growth

Within the last chapter, I provided you with an intimate snapshot of how I applied the first five steps to activating lasting change. You have learned about my acknowledgments, assessments, and actions required to move towards the peak level of growth within Maslow's Hierarchy of Needs, Self-fulfillment. It may seem like a quick transformation when evaluated in this way, but I cannot express enough the amount of time, dedication, and work required to pull me out of the destructive state I slipped into during COVID-19. Any journey of growth that is actively pursued will be uncomfortable and, at times, feel unbearable, as it requires you to consistently step out of your comfort zone over a long period of time. There are many more unknowns to this world than there are known; to truly accomplish living an enlightened life, we must constantly step out into the unfamiliar.

This chapter will review how I applied the sixth step of activating lasting change during COVID-19: *Review and Assess.* As I share the results of engaging my plans for elevation over the last two years, I hope it can inspire you to boldly and courageously seek the change you desire to live your best life. It is critical to note that these results are merely the beginning phases of what I intend to create. I am not stopping here, as there are no final destinations on the journey to living a purposeful life. Now let's take a look at the results within each level of growth.

Basic Needs: Physiological & Safety Needs

Physiological Needs

As you have learned in the previous chapter, a lack of sleep and physical deterioration of my body due to anxiety and gym closures were the primary threats to my basic physical needs. I uncovered the changes required to elevate my physiological necessities by completing the detailed 6W question sequence. If you recall, the SMART goals I established to enhance this level of needs included:

Sleep: I will get seven hours of sleep every night after one month of going to bed at 10 pm.

Anxiety: I will begin overcoming my fears after three months of working with my anxiety coach every Tuesday at 8 pm.

Physical Health: I will reach elevated physical health within three months of committing to 45-minute workouts five days a week.

As I implemented these new goals into my life, I made alterations to them as transformations began to unfold. It's essential to recognize that adjusting your objectives along the journey of elevation is normal and constructive. The outcomes of applying these goals and the tweaks made along the way included:

Sleep: It took closer to three months to achieve a minimum of 7 hours of sleep. I also added a daily thirty-minute nap in the afternoon while my kids napped. Although this goal took longer to achieve, I still accomplished it, resulting in abundant energy.

Anxiety: As I regularly reached out to my anxiety coach and applied her teachings, I noticed a significant improvement in three months. However, it took me about twelve months to establish a healthy and positive state of mind.

Physical Health: After three months of committing to 45-minute workouts five days a week, I manifested a physique in its entirety that reached a level of fitness I had never experienced before. I had surpassed my expectations with my physical health. To maintain this level of health, I have infused this new exercise routine as a part of my healthy lifestyle.

Persistently applying these goals over time resulted in the complete achievement of meeting my physiological needs. I can say wholeheartedly that my physiological needs were eventually met in all areas, contributing to a solid foundation for growth in other areas of my life.

Safety Needs

My personal safety needs, composed of physical and economic aspects, experienced significant growth throughout the pandemic. Because these necessities are deeply connected to one's mental processes, my assessments completed included this factor as I established my goals. I distinguished the differences between actual safety threats vs. the false threats my mind made up due to my thought processes. The objective I set to meet my safety needs included:

Physical Safety: Committing to thirty minutes of research every day to understand the virus and vaccine over one month will enhance my knowledge of the risks associated with both.

Job & Financial Security: I will eliminate the fears of job and financial security concerns by applying the four-step process to elevating my thoughts, reading an educational book for fifteen minutes a day, and listening to a podcast daily over three months.

Personal Security: I will spend fifteen minutes a day educating myself about an individual's protected rights and freedoms for one month.

As I applied the actions identified to enhance my safety needs, I began to imprint the facts vs. the fears into my cognitive narratives. The timeline to achieve the fulfillment of these actions varied as such:

Physical Safety: Prioritizing thirty minutes of researching the virus and vaccine every day over one month brought clarity and understanding to my concerns. This enlightenment brought peace and confidence to my decisions made. I decided to continue my education regularly around the virus and the vaccine as research evolved.

Job & Financial Security: Applying the four-step process to transforming my thoughts, reading an educational book for fifteen minutes, and listening to a podcast daily positively impacted my thoughts, including those around job and financial security. Kelsey and I also created a plan to ensure continued progress towards our financial goals to reduce my anxieties around these concerns. This action plan included expanding my coaching business into the online space and partnering with my sister, Kayla, who is an incredible wealth and lifestyle design coach.

Personal Security: After prioritizing fifteen minutes a day to understand an individual's protected rights and freedoms for one month, I significantly increased the understanding of my rights as a Canadian citizen. I continued this goal for six additional months to enhance my security even more. Another action Kelsey and I added to this goal was to develop a list of potential locations we would consider relocating to if we experienced any further impacts on our personal rights and freedoms.

These actions led to the fading of the following fears regarding my safety needs: COVID-19 virus, the different developmental vaccines, loss of my family's supporting income, and limitations on our nation's rights and freedom. You may have noticed that I used the word fading when describing the changes in the strength of these fears experienced. This word choice is deliberate because if I am not consciously controlling my cognitive processes, these anxieties will begin to flourish once again. I have experienced moments where these fears regarding my safety flare up, and I am again consumed with worry. The key here is that I have developed an awareness of these psychological processes, and I now know what it takes to rewire them. The outcome of this is my negative thoughts last a day or two rather than months at a time. To continue to live free from these fears, I am consistently elevating my psychological needs, as you will learn more about in this next section.

Psychological Needs: Social & Esteem Needs

Social Needs

The overwhelming sense of division and separation I experienced through COVID-19 fueled one of my greatest yearnings: the need for connection and unity. To satisfy these needs, I came up with the following actions within my thought processes and environment:

Thought Processes: I will diligently apply the four-step process of autosuggestion fifteen minutes a day over three months to achieve success in rewiring my thoughts. As a result, I will begin to feel more deeply connected to God and others around me. Again, this will be supported by reading a personal growth book for fifteen minutes daily and listening to an enlightening podcast daily.

Outer Environment: I will begin to reach out to family and friends and prioritize connecting with one individual weekly for three months to elevate my social needs.

I noticed my social needs beginning to heal by diligently applying these goals. I could feel the internal and external divisions starting to fuse. The following results had occurred:

Thought Processes: Through my actions of consistently following through with my healthy daily inputs of reading and listening to personal growth audios, I began to connect with my faith pillar more intimately. One of the books I read was a spiritual book, *There's a Spiritual Solution to Every Problem,* by Wayne Dyer. This book opened my eyes to the connectedness all around me. I realized that I do not need to rely solely on the presence of physical bodies to feel this sense of unity. It doesn't mean that I don't appreciate and enjoy connections with other beings; it simply means that I have additional ways to fulfill and support this need. This realization truly opened my heart and mind to receiving the unity that already exists in the universe, the limitless, expansive energy that flows through all.

Outer Environment: As I released the expectation placed upon others to fulfill this need, my relationships began to flourish, strengthening my relationship pillar. By consciously reaching out to family and friends at least once a week for three months, it became a new habitual way of life for me. Through prioritizing valuable connections in my life, I began to experience the authenticity of meaningful relationships.

With all of this said, it is essential to acknowledge that feeling alone still occurs in my life, but now it is primarily due to the moments of weakness within my faith rather than the absence of an individual. This outcome was one of my most impactful experiences throughout the Coronavirus Pandemic.

Esteem Needs

Becoming consciously aware of my psychological processes and understanding the significant influences on my belief system,

I was able to establish meaningful goals that would ultimately transform the nature of my experiences and outcomes. If you recall, the four significant impacts on an individual's beliefs are Inner Dialogue, Stimulus & Energy Levels, Self-Esteem & Egotism, and Ignorance & Knowledge. Using these four components as a framework, I established some meaningful goals to elevate my esteem needs. You may notice redundancy with some of these goals set. Still, to show you the entire evaluation I completed, I will share all the goals I have identified at the esteem level of needs.

> ***Inner Dialogue***: I will spend fifteen minutes a day consciously applying the four-step process of reprograming my mind. I will also commit to reading fifteen minutes a day from an educational book and listening to a podcast daily for three months.

> ***Stimulus & Energy Levels:*** To ensure the entirety of my energy levels improve, I had set a goal for each of the three energy zones.

>> *Cognitive Energy Zone:* Goals to elevate my mental energy zone are the same as those I have shared for improving my Inner Dialogue.

>> *Physical Energy Zone:* I will enhance my physical energy levels within three months of committing to a healthy exercise regime encompassing 45-minute workouts five days a week.

>> *Environmental Energy Zone:* I will elevate my environmental energy levels by eliminating the energy leaks in my surroundings over the next three months.

Self-Esteem & Egotism: After three months of consistently applying the four-step process, reading a book for fifteen minutes a day, and listening to a personal development podcast daily, I will reduce and eliminate the ego in my life.

Ignorance & Knowledge: After one month of prioritizing thirty minutes a day to become educated about both the vaccine and the virus and fifteen minutes a day to enhance my understanding of the charter of rights and freedoms, I will enhance my overall knowledge contributing to the elevation of my esteem needs.

To capture the significance of the transformations at this level, I will share the outcomes experienced within each of the four significant impacts on an individual's belief system. By elevating these influences, I could improve the entirety of my esteem needs.

Inner Dialogue: By applying the four-step process, reading an educational book fifteen minutes a day, and listening to a podcast daily, my self-speech and inner thoughts began to transform. I experienced a transition from a fixed mindset laden with fear to one of being open and exuding hope. As my mind became susceptible to change, so did my subconscious thoughts. This state of evolution was the turning point for me; as I controlled my thoughts, I began to control the outcomes in my life.

Stimulus & Energy Levels: Applying the goals I established for each of the three energy zones resulted in a significant improvement in my energy levels.

Cognitive Energy Zone: As I transformed my thoughts, my mental energies naturally began to elevate. Soon, my cognitive energy zone became abundantly full of energy, spilling over into my other energy zones, the physical and environmental.

Physical Energy Zone: As you have learned earlier, I surpassed my goals of achieving a healthy physique by committing to forty-five-minute workouts five days a week over three months. The result of this has led to optimum physical energy levels.

Environmental Energy Zone: Adjusting the environmental influences on my energy levels involved setting boundaries with specific activities, individuals, and inputs. I stopped: watching the news, reading news articles, watching negative TV shows, and listening to toxic podcasts. This elevated environment became a bodyguard for my cognitive process. It gave me the security to work on the lower energy thoughts that already plagued my mind without being concerned with additional negative influences adding to the energy leaks. I soon found myself surrounded by positive and growth-infused environments and encouraging individuals. This abundance of energy in my environment began to flow outward toward my family and community.

Self-Esteem & Egotism: The journey of shifting my inner dialogue and thoughts to those of a higher frequency, as described earlier, is the very same actions I took to reduce and eliminate the egoic thoughts that developed throughout COVID-19. The four-step process I applied daily involved: creating awareness of the egoic thoughts present, being willing to alter these thoughts, establishing new and empowering thoughts, and reading these affirmations daily. Through this process, I realized that I will always need to be working on eliminating the unhealthy grips that ego has over my life, especially during uncertain and chaotic times. Life is full of unexpected moments, and if we choose to halt our efforts to move toward our higher selves, the unhealthy ego will likely begin to emerge. Any moments of division from our best selves can create a fertile environment that spawns thoughts of self-importance. Through studying the many faces of egotism present in my life, I became aware of their entanglement with one another. The natural consequence of exterminating one expression of ego led to an environment where I could eliminate all forms of egotism.

Accumulation & Ownership of Things: I learned to mentally let go of my material attachments by recognizing that these items do not define who I am. My faith journey helped open my mind and heart to accepting that I am a spiritual being, free from attachment.

Achievements and Weaknesses: Working through my misidentification to achievements, I learned the principle that being attached to nothing is a prerequisite to being open to new possibilities. This openness has led to new opportunities, moving me toward my purpose. Take writing this book, for example; I am not a writer, but I am someone who has something to say with the hopes of positively making an impact in people's lives. I would never have considered writing a book if I didn't learn to open myself up to the abundance of possibilities that are out there.

Personality & Reputation: The need to uphold a notable reputation or the desire to appease others throughout COVID-19 led to a misalignment between my actions and my key-value pillars. By refocusing on my purpose, values, and desires, I built the courage to break free from the chains of people-pleasing. I learned that if I do not dictate the outcomes of my life, someone else will. I also realized that to experience the external results of peace and freedom from superficial judgments; I had to go inward to do the challenging work on my own critical mind first. The outcome of my vulnerability and commitment to growth as I elevated my thinking was liberating. For the first time since the pandemic began two years ago, as I write this, I have made every decision through my values system, free from the external pull of appeasing others. I had reached the utmost freedom I have experienced, and it was all due to the mental release that transpired as I chose to step up and write my own story, hand in hand with God. With this release, I began to notice the fear of raising my kids during this time melt away. This courage created a ripple effect, where my son also began to enjoy life again. His child-like spirit began to emerge, where curiosity fueled his desire to expand his outer world.

Physical Attributes: The most rewarding part of my entire fitness journey occurred when the pandemic began. For the first time, I learned to slow down, and I became entirely open to other avenues of health and fitness. I applied the teachings of yoga, pilates, kickboxing, and stretching in addition to my weight training. As I combined my mental and physical health throughout my training sessions, I learned to accept my body as it was designed.

Separation: Eliminating my critical and judgmental state of mind was one of the most exhaustive processes I had experienced throughout the Coronavirus Pandemic. This was because I needed to walk through my own fears and judgments, taking the time to understand the roots of them and dealing with my emotions of shame and guilt after realizing the thoughts that I was experiencing. Through overcoming my egotistical thoughts full of dichotomies, I learned that my judgments are simply a reflection of the critical views that I held towards myself. Over time, I released these negative thought patterns and instilled thoughts of love, compassion, and understanding towards myself and others. Resultantly, I developed a stronger connection with those around me.

Independence from God: As you have learned throughout the pages of this book, my experience through the COVID pandemic led to a complete transformation of my faith, leading to a spiritual awakening. This part of my journey had the most profound impact on my path toward self-fulfillment because it brought me closer to living a purposeful life in alignment with God. I can now show and feel utmost gratitude for the events that did unfold, including the darkest days that my family experienced. It is very complex to explain these unseen experiences and knowing's to the world. All I can say is that when things become dark and quiet enough, you become susceptible to tuning into the forces outside of yourself. These moments fulfilled my desire to truly know God, not just the knowledge of the great divinity that exists in all of us. This spiritual awakening required me to walk this dark and lonely path to experience the significance and impact of the light within. I now accept there exists an internal illumination that is a part of who I am, regardless of outside circumstances. I can now say with certainty that I know God.

Ignorance & Knowledge: Acknowledging that I don't know everything has been one of my greatest lifelines throughout this trying time. It has opened me up to receiving new information to make educated and informed decisions rather than those out of fear and ego. This openness allowed me to question things with courage and make thoughtful decisions aligned with my purpose, values, and vision. After one month of educating myself about both the vaccine and the virus for thirty minutes a day and fifteen minutes a day to understand the rights and freedoms, I gained a significant amount of knowledge about these topics. My fears faded as factual-based information led to courage, peace, and understanding.

Self-Actualization Needs

The outcome of manifesting abundance within my basic and psychological needs led to a sturdy foundation required before moving on towards self-fulfillment. As I took steps towards a higher awareness, my vision began to open up and shine brighter and brighter, forging a pull so strong that my aspirations expanded beyond myself. I began to look for ways to positively influence my community. As you have learned, I chose to step up my coaching business to the online space to increase my impact across the globe. Additionally, I was guided to write this book, with a sincere hope that its teachings can help make this world a better place. It was never my passion or dream to be a writer, but it is my vision to make an impact on every soul. As we go on this journey together, I hope you will be positively enlightened and impacted as I am writing it. When your purpose includes positively influencing those around you, you have entered self-actualization.

"Every action we take impacts the lives of others around us. The question is, are you aware of your impacts?" ~Arthur Carmazzi

CHAPTER 12

Your Impact: Unifying Our Families, Communities, and Our Nations

Together, we have walked through this journey of what it looks like to elevate your life, transforming yourself into the highest version of who you desire to be. Imagine you have done all the work you set out to accomplish, taking one step at a time. I am now going to challenge you to turn around and look at the path you have walked. What will you see, hear or feel? The answer to this question will be unique to your journey, but one thing I know for certain is that the dark or shaded path you were once on is now illuminated with light. The next question now becomes, what is the impact of the light you have created in your life on others around you?

The Collective Cognitive Energy Zone

We have discussed the intricacies of the mind and its power to determine the outcome of your life. You and no one else has control of your thoughts, meaning you have the ability to foster, alter and grow your mental processes. You have discovered that any thought that enters your conscious mind, once infused with emotions, becomes the dominating belief in your subconscious mind. This thought and emotion loop then determines your vibrations or energy level in your cognitive energy zone, leading to your actions and outcomes. If you recall, we reviewed this process in Chapter 4, which is called the Belief Cycle. I have summarized this process below in Figure 7.

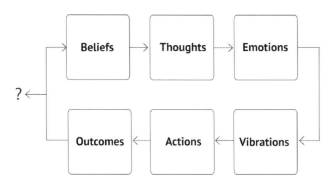

Figure 7: Belief Cycle

The energy flowing from step to step can be transformed and altered but never destroyed. So, what happens when we get to the outcomes of this cycle? We know energy cannot vanish, so it must go somewhere. This energy can flow in a few different directions, including back into your belief cycle. The other direction this energy can flow is outward to your physical and environmental energy zones, as shown in Figure 8.

Figure 8: Energy Flow from Your Cognitive Zone to Your Environmental Zone

When we transform our thoughts to operate at high frequencies, in alignment with those of the universal energy, we can encourage these energies to expand, eventually flowing outward from this energy zone. The result of this expansion and overflow from the mind is the elevation of our physical energy zone. As we go to work plugging the energy leaks that may reside in our physical zone, we experience transcendence within our bodies. As our physical energy fills up, it will begin to overflow into our environment. Here, the impact of one person's energy can transcend an entire family, community, nation, and ultimately our world. Let's consider looking at a three-tiered water fountain, as shown in Figure 9, to help establish the connection between all three of these energy zones.

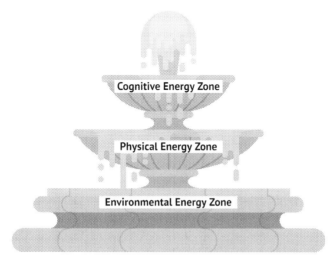

Figure 9: Intricacies of Our Energy Zones

As the water builds up in the first tier, eventually, it begins to spill over into the second tier if there are no leaks. As the second tier begins to capture water, it will rise, eventually spilling over to the third tier. This process is a fantastic analogy of how our energy zones interact; as one zone experiences an abundance of energy, it begins to expand outwards to the other zones. This connectedness vividly shows the need to monitor and care for our energy levels, whether they are a part of our minds, bodies, or environments.

Collective Environmental Energy Zone

So how does this overflow of energy from our mind and body impact our surroundings? Our primary environments consist of our homes and our communities. Our communities are composed of our work, activities, and places of worship. Naturally, an overflow of energy from our physical energy zone will first flow into our homes, impacting our immediate family. As the family unit elevates, the outward energy flow moves into our communities and countries, eventually impacting our world. Refer to Figure 10 to visually see the energy flow from our cognitive energy zone. As you can see, because of our intricate connections to one another, one person's willingness to elevate, grow and change can ultimately transcend the globe.

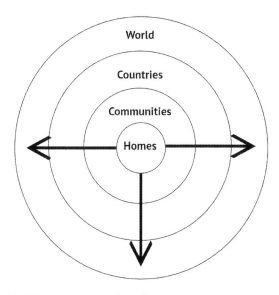

Figure 10: Energy Expansion from Our Homes to Our Globe

A remarkable parallel to our connectedness is the interactions of the neurons in our brains. On their own, without the electrical signals flowing through them, they are simply a group of neurons. Now, if we add electrical impulses or energy through one of the neurons, it does not just disappear; it has to go somewhere. Gaps between each neuron, called synapses, allow for the conduction of energy to flow from one neuron to the next. They become a connected unit operating as one, the nervous system. One can see a neuron on its own has potential, but a group of neurons working as one is powerful. Much like the nervous system, energy flows from one individual to the next, operating as a unit. I like to call this magnificent flow of energy that divinely connects one individual to the next, Source, God, or Universe, but you can call it whatever you want. One of us standing alone has potential, but the group of us divinely connected is omnipotent.

Perhaps you never considered the gravity of your thoughts and actions and their impact on a global scale until now. As our personal belief cycles influence and contribute to the beliefs adopted by society, a conclusion can be established that there must also be a collective beliefs process, as shown in Figure 11.

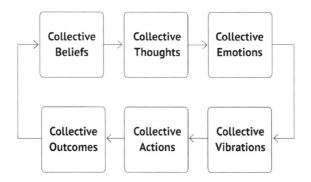

Figure 11: The Collective Belief Process

This diagram shows that our collective thoughts will determine the collective outcome we will experience throughout our globe. This united belief cycle held by society has always existed, whether in prosperous or trying times. In times of uncertainty, the pre-existing toxicity within an individual's mind becomes exposed and magnified, as exemplified during the Coronavirus pandemic. During unfortunate events such as this, it is more important than ever for us to step up and take responsibility for the one thing we can all control our belief cycle. Because if we don't, we will lead ourselves down the path of destruction, destroying all the good within our homes, communities, and nations. Let's take a look at the collective state of our world during COVID-19 to help bring clarity to the path many individuals are embarking upon. With this assessment, you will be exposed to the potential outcomes that may occur if things do not change.

The Negative Collective: Belief Cycle

We have looked at how our higher frequency energies abundantly flow from our minds outwardly to our external environments. A similar occurrence happens with the lower frequency energies of the ego. Once a mind is poisoned with self-importance, these lower vibrations begin to drip through the cracks into our physical energy zone and eventually into our environment. We can use the fountain example to help show this, but this time, instead of the water abundantly overflowing the edges of each tier, the water slips through cracks that have been formed in the fountain walls. These cracks represent the energy leaks in our lives that permit our lower selves to dominate.

Looking at the current state of our world today, early in the year 2022, it is evident that our lower selves are dominating our collective thoughts. Since the emergence of COVID-19, statistics show a 273% increase in mental health issues of anxiety and depression reported, encompassing around 41% of the population[1]. This jump in psychological concerns only shows the severe and reported cases. Many more individuals than this likely suffer from the lower energy thoughts that have taken over our minds. So, what is the cause of this massive shift? Our cognitive processes determine our mental health; lower energy thoughts and emotions will create poor mental health conditions, leading to anxieties and depression. Figure 12 summarizes the dominating thought processes throughout the pandemic. As one can see, the results of our collective thinking across our world during COVID-19 has been devastating. This destruction is because our collective egotism dominates our thoughts of spirituality, love, compassion, joy, servitude, and abundance.

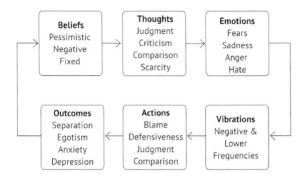

Figure 12: Negative Belief Process

To summarize the current state of our world, in Wayne's words, "ego strives to keep the populous nervously on the edge, with reminders to view the world in terms of us vs. them. It is insane to believe that anyone who does not fit into our tribal mentality is a potential enemy." [2] These profound words mean that egoic thoughts of separation lead to individuals believing that their way of life is the only way, and to live any differently means you are less of a person and even a threat. This thinking pattern causes all of our problems in this world. Our society, dominated by ego, strives to conform all of humanity into a single mold representing the ideal citizen. This conformity goes against our natural state of creation, where we are all unique in our ways. The outcome of this pressure leads to the toxic component of ego oozing out of those who can no longer handle the strains. In addition to the Coronavirus Pandemic, we are also confronting a collective ego pandemic.

The Positive Collective: Belief Cycle

We all must stop for a moment and ask ourselves if we are OK with the outcomes and events that have transpired in our world today? Are we OK allowing things to unfold the way they are?

Would you be at peace leaving your children and grandchildren to grow up in this world we live in? If your answer to any of these questions is NO, then the time is now to start making some changes. It all starts with you raising your thought frequencies towards your higher self. If we can all join together on this journey, you will see the following unfold in Figure 13:

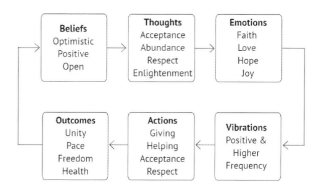

Figure 13: Positive Belief Process

Imagine a world where we are educated on the power of our thoughts, knowing that we can truly achieve the outcomes shared in Figure 13. I think back to my educational years, and I do not recall learning about the belief cycle or our ability to make this world a better place just through thought alone. If our school systems adopted these teachings, our world would be significantly different from today. Individuals would learn that when you operate in alignment with your highest self, you will profoundly impact those around you. You would discover that your presence alone will have an indestructible power, including some of the below impacts.

- Your presence will shine light in areas of darkness, raising the energy levels of those around you. This elevation will lead others to feel enlightened and connected, never alone.

- The optimistic energy that flows outwards from yourself will neutralize the negative thoughts that may exist in other individuals' minds. You will help others feel good about themselves, leaving a lasting impression. Your positivity may trigger their own mental reboot, inspiring those around you to pursue greatness and live purposefully through their values.
- Your internal contentment will help others find peace in moments of their own turmoil and sickness, which will help them open up and move towards tranquility and health.
- Through being open, trusting, and accepting, you will create an environment of this exact nature. Consequently, you will lead others to open their hearts allowing themselves to be free from the chains of society and step courageously into their true nature.

Your profound impact is not to be taken for granted or viewed as an insignificant matter. We are all world changers the moment we choose to be our best selves. Regardless of the adversities, you may face, you must remain diligent in being the light in the room. On your growth journey, you must remember that you will experience individuals that operate out of their lower selves and choose to stay there. Your transformations will become the mirror others hold up to themselves, encouraging them to self-reflect on their journey. And if they are not ready for a change in their life, you may experience their resistance in the form of judgment and criticism. The key here is that this is not a reflection of you but rather a reflection of who they chose to be. At all costs, remain in alignment with your highest self, and you will be rewarded with a legacy of positive impact.

"Naysayers have little power over us – unless we give it to them." ~ Arianna Huffington

CHAPTER 13

Reflecting on Your Journey

In this final chapter, my goal is to bring together everything you have learned, showing you the clear path to your desired outcome. Once you are confident of the direction you must go, you will be inspired to take the transformational action required. This clarity will paint a visual of your future self, walking in the shoes of the best version of you. Let's step back to the beginning pages of this book, where we talk about the six critical steps for lasting change.

As you have learned, the first step that is foundational to change is having a *Purpose Fueled by a Burning Desire* to transform your current reality. At this moment, I am going to ask you to step into the future version of you that is one, three, or five years down the road from now. Contemplate what you want this future version of you to look like. What will you have, what will you do, and who will you be? Now, declare your mission statement that embodies your purpose, key values, and desires. How do you feel as you boldly claim this future for yourself? Hold on to these emotions and remember them every day. These feelings will be one of your motivating factors driving change in alignment with the new you.

Now I am going to ask you to snap back to the present moment, in the now. Take in your surroundings, thoughts, emotions, actions, and outcomes. What does your life look like? How did you get to where you are at? Who is present in your life? As you ask these questions, this is where you begin Step 2 of activating lasting change, *Taking an Inventory*. Take your past and present evaluations as deeply as you are willing to go. Use various tools such as the Belief Cycle, Maslow's Hierarchy of Needs, your Key Pillars, and the 6W Series of Questions to bring depth to your understandings and clarity to your present state.

Next, I am going to ask you to step into owning your past and present so you can begin to own your future. This accountability action is the third step to creating lasting change: *Take Ownership*. Declare "my present moment is a collection of the actions and behaviors I chose in my past. These outcomes do not define me, but rather I define them. Now that I have accepted full responsibility for my past and present, I can stand up and claim my future".

Through accepting accountability for every outcome, you have endured, you are now ready to take the brave step forward into *Creating a Plan and Taking Action*. Once again, I want you to step into the future version of yourself, your highest version of you. Again, take in all your senses; what do you see, hear, and feel? Who are you in that ideal moment? What does this future you look like? Now step back into the current moment, and ask yourself, "how can I get to this future version of me?" This moment is where you begin to map out the path you will take to move from where you are to where you desire to be. Ensure you lean on the inventory you have taken in step two of this process to formulate a specific, measurable, attainable, relevant, and time-bound plan so that your goals are SMART and set up for success.

As you begin to take steps forward, you will start to feel motivated, energized, excited, and hopeful for what the future holds. Your thoughts will be vibrating at high frequencies, and you will begin to attach to your desired outcomes emotionally. These new thoughts and emotions start to rewire your psychological programming. As you make significant progress, you may find a part of you with doubts, worries, or concerns. I want you to pause in these moments and step into them. Ask yourself, what obstacles or roadblocks are beginning to appear? Is it the fear of failure, dependency, lack of persistence, approval-seeking, procrastination, or a different perceived roadblock? This moment is where you will utilize Step 5: *Overcoming Obstacles.* It is essential to acknowledge that roadblocks will happen, as they are a normal part of the journey to elevation. I encourage you to affirm that obstacles signify that you are transforming; you must experience a breakdown before you are shown the breakthrough.

The final component to activating lasting change, Step 6, is completing regular *Reviews and Assessments.* To ensure that the alterations you are making are moving you closer to your desired future self, I will invite you to take moments of pause along your journey of growth and development. Here I encourage you to walk through the exercise of stepping into the desired you one, three, or five years down the road. Take in the picture you see and the results you will have. Then step back into the present, and ask, "am I moving towards my desired self?" Only you will know whether you are moving in the right direction. Recognize that these self-reflections are meant to bring awareness to your current situation so that you can course-correct along your journey. You must let go of self-judgment and condemnation if you veer off the path. We are often our worst critics, and by allowing these negative thoughts to enter our minds, we self-destruct, wiping the progress we have made. I encourage you to enter this transformation process knowing that this growth journey is not about perfection but rather about progression, becoming one percent better every day.

Final Words

My vision for you and all of humanity is to find our way in this world surrounded by love, peace, harmony, abundance, joy, gratitude, empathy, and many more thoughts aligned with God. To do this, we must first look within before we can clearly see the path we are destined to be on. And once you find that path, your brightness will illuminate the paths of others around you, bringing clarity into their lives. Your outright changes in this outrageous world may be the very thing that transforms it.

ENDNOTES

Chapter 1

1. *Wayne Dyer - Learn to Die While You Are Alive*. (2008b, November 30). [Video]. YouTube. https://www.youtube.com/watch?v=iZGK3jf0v9s

Chapter 2

1. Hannah Ritchie, Edouard Mathieu, Lucas Rodés-Guirao, Cameron Appel, Charlie Giattino, Esteban Ortiz-Ospina, Joe Hasell, Bobbie Macdonald, Diana Beltekian and Max Roser (2020) - "Coronavirus Pandemic (COVID-19)". *Published online at OurWorldInData.org*. Retrieved from: https://ourworldindata.org/coronavirus
2. House, J. S., Landis, K. R., & Umberson, D. (1988). Social Relationships and Health. *Science*, *241*(4865), 540–545. https://doi.org/10.1126/science.3399889

Chapter 3

1. D. (2021). *The Power of Intention by Dyer, Dr. Wayne W. (2005) Paperback*. Hay House Inc.
2. Maslow, A.H. (1943*). A Theory of Human Motivation.* In Psychological Review, 50 (4), 430-437.

Chapter 4

1. *Do sharks hunt people? Most sharks are not dangerous to humans — people are not part of their natural diet.* (n.d.). National Ocean Service. https://oceanservice.noaa.gov/facts/sharkseat.html
2. Hershberger, M. (2021, September 14). *4 ways science can help you overcome your fear of sharks.* Matador Network. https://matadornetwork.com/bnt/4-ways-science-fear-sharks/
3. Dispenza, J. (2013). *Breaking The Habit of Being Yourself: How to Lose Your Mind and Create a New One* (Reprint ed.). Hay House Inc.
4. Hill, N., & Pell, A. (2005). *Think and Grow Rich: The Landmark Bestseller--Now Revised and Updated for the 21st Century* (Rev Exp ed.). Tarcher.
5. Robins, T. *Reprogram Your Mind: Understand and Take Control of the Subconscious Mind.* Retrieved from https://www.tonyrobbins.com/mind-meaning/how-to-reprogram-your-mind/
6. Yalom, I. D. (1980). *Existential Psychotherapy* (1st ed.). Basic Books.
7. U.S. Census Bureau [Producer]. (2020-2022). *Indicators of Anxiety or Depression Based on Reported Frequency of Symptoms* [Data Set]. National Center for Health Statistics

[Distributor]. https://www.cdc.gov/nchs/covid19/pulse/
mental-health.htm

Chapter 5

1. Watkins, M. (2021, November 23). *How Drugs Affect the Brain & Central Nervous System.* American Addiction Centers. https://americanaddictioncenters. org/health-complications-addiction/central-nervous-system
2. Worley S. L. (2018). *The Extraordinary Importance of Sleep: The Detrimental Effects of Inadequate Sleep on Health and Public Safety Drive an Explosion of Sleep Research.* P & T : a peer-reviewed journal for formulary management, 43(12), 758–763. Retrieved from https://www.ncbi.nlm.nih.gov/pmc/articles/PMC6281147/
3. Orth, U., Robins, R. W., & Meier, L. L. (2009). Disentangling the effects of low self-esteem and stressful events on depression: Findings from three longitudinal studies. *Journal of Personality and Social Psychology,* 97(2), 307–321. https://doi.org/10.1037/a0015645
4. *Ego - Definition, Meaning & Synonyms.* (n.d.). Vocabulary. Com. Retrieved February 15, 2022, from https://www.vocabulary.com/dictionary/ego
5. D. (2021). *The Power of Intention by Dyer, Dr. Wayne W. (2005) Paperback.* Hay House Inc.

Chapter 8

1. Hannah Ritchie, Edouard Mathieu, Lucas Rodés-Guirao, Cameron Appel, Charlie Giattino, Esteban Ortiz-Ospina, Joe Hasell, Bobbie Macdonald, Diana Beltekian and Max

Roser (2020) - "Coronavirus Pandemic (COVID-19)". *Published online at OurWorldInData.org.* Retrieved from: https://ourworldindata.org/coronavirus

2. Taylor, B. (2006). *Poverty & Crime - Fundamental Finance.* Copyright 2007. Retrieved December 1, 2021, from http://economics.fundamentalfinance.com/povertycrime.php

Chapter 9

1. Dyer, W. W. (2001). *Your Erroneous Zones: Step-by-Step Advice for Escaping the Trap of Negative Thinking and Taking Control of Your Life* (First ed.). William Morrow Paperbacks.

Chapter 12

1. Terlizzi EP, Schiller JS. *Estimates of mental health symptomatology, by month of interview: United States,* 2019. National Center for Health Statistics. March 2021. Retrieved from: https://www.cdc.gov/nchs/data/nhis/mental-health-monthly-508.pdf
U.S. Census Bureau [Producer].. (2020-2022). *Indicators of Anxiety or Depression Based on Reported Frequency of Symptoms* [Data Set]. National Center for Health Statistics [Distributor]. https://www.cdc.gov/nchs/covid19/pulse/mental-health.htm

2. Dyer, W. (April 28,2017). *How to Control Your Ego.* Retrieved from https://www.youtube.com/watch?v=ploeoqfRUCw&t=100s

INDEX

266

Printed in the United States
by Baker & Taylor Publisher Services